FORGOS OF THE EGO

A NOVEL BY

IFEANYI E. ILUKWE

FORGOS OF THE EGO

Copyright ©2023 by Ifeanyi Ilukwe

All rights reserved.

No part of this publication may be reproduced, distributed, or transmitted in any form or by any means, including photocopying, recording, or other electronic or mechanical methods, without the prior written permission of the publisher, except in the case of brief quotations embodied in critical reviews and certain other non-commercial uses permitted by copyright law.

For permissions requests or inquiries, please contact: ifeanyiilukwe@gmail.com

First Paperback Edition August 2023.

To Ada, my anchor, and Daniella, Malia, Alexa, and David, my inspiration. Your love fuels this work.

And

In loving memory of Mrs. Justina O. Okeke (Nee Onwura), a legacy of strength.

The Perils of Pride

The Perils of Pride, a weighty sin,

A trap that snares both heart and skin,

An all-consuming, toxic pride,

That wounds the soul and hardens the hide.

It starts so small, a little boast,

A tiny pride that swells the most,

And then it grows, it takes control,

A cancerous growth within the soul.

And when it's mixed with spiritual pride,

It poisons our hearts, and truth it hides,

It blinds our eyes to other's pain,

And leads us to a path of disdain.

For in our arrogance, we think we're right,

And close our ears to wisdom's light,

We think ourselves above the rest,

And judge them harshly with no request.

The Perils of Pride, a deadly foe,

A cancer that can quickly grow,

But there is hope, a different way,

A path that leads to a brighter day.

For in humility, we find,

Strength of heart and peace of mind,

A way to live, a way to be,

That sets our spirit truly free.

So let us heed the warning clearly,

And from the path of pride steer clear,

For in humility, we'll find,

The peace and joy of heart and mind.

Ifeanyi Ilukwe©.

Prologue

When the people who live there have affection for their city, they refer to it as "The 6ix," which gives the place a lot more personality. The city of Toronto in the 21st century is a complex pattern of colours that demonstrate the vitality of multiculturalism. Its expansive horizons are suitable for the creation of works of art by dreamers and are nourished by aspiration.

People on their way to their destinations are roused from sleep each morning by the sun's rays as they travel through the streets like arteries, and you can't miss them as dawn breaks each day. Streetcars float gracefully above the bustling avenues below where cars are whizzing by at high speeds. At this city's pulsating core beats the heart—the soul embodied within its denizens arriving from globally divergent places carrying stories, customs, and treasures that make up the mosaic of cultures defining "The 6ix" in all its glory.

A trip to Toronto isn't truly worthwhile unless you get to see the city's iconic skyscrapers, which are typically made of glass and steel and appear to be pointing in the direction of the moon. It is an ecosystem of commerce that is bustling with innovative minds ranging from business owners to creatives all working together in unison to have a positive impact on the transformation of the world.

On the other side of these strange giants is a lake that looks like it hasn't been touched by people. The shimmering waters of Ontario gently lap onto shores that are bordered by peaceful verdant parks, providing this fascinating city with an oasis of tranquilly in the midst of the hustle and bustle of everyday life.

The city of Toronto would not be the same without its thriving artistic community. Grand theatres resound with symphonic melodies that captivate audiences with performances from various cultures that make them laugh and applaud. Galleries are filled with improbable pieces of creative expressionism that stir our imaginations.

When night falls over "The 6ix," towers with flashing lights light up the skyline, giving the impression that a rainbow is taking place beneath a blanket of stars with colours emerging from every corner. Visitors have the option of exploring secret underground museums housed in buildings that don't appear to be much of anything, or they can go on a scenic walk-through elevated bars that offer views of Toronto's glowing tapestry.

In Toronto, all are welcome to create cherished memories amidst an atmosphere filled with music and laughter. This city serves as a prime example of boundless potential at play through collaboration while maintaining one's inner balance. To call Toronto merely a hub would be unjustified- it breathes life into every citizen's spirit, fueling their aspirations whilst never forgetting about their pursuit of ever elusive contentment in life.

 Unlike other Canadian cities, "The 6ix" represents not only physical location but also embodies an idea- an idea which urges individuals to fight against all odds, making the most out of every opportunity that presents itself along the way without ever giving up on hope for what lies beyond. This captivating haven calms adventurous souls with its dynamic ambience and boundless prospects.

On a quiet street in the suburbs, there was a charming house where people could go to get away from the busy world. Its brick exterior had a timeless appeal, and the lawns and flowering gardens added a touch of natural beauty. As the golden light of the morning sun shone on the neighbourhood, He got himself ready for another day of work in the warm kitchen as the rising sun cast its golden light upon the surrounding area.

The aroma of freshly brewed coffee drifted through the air, providing him with a sense of calm that he savoured with each sip before painstakingly preparing his hearty breakfast in order to fuel his day. He hurriedly collected his keys and then entered his sleek silver sedan, which began to make a melodious purring sound as it merged onto the bustling city streets once he had completed his preparations.

While he was on his way to work, he witnessed a shifting scene of tall buildings stretching up into a sky that was filled with dawn. In addition to this, he drove through intricate roads that were woven into an urban landscape and allowed for the smooth movement of streams of vehicles. Soon after, he showed up at his workplace, which was a gleaming tower made of glass and steel that represented innovation and was a place where ideas were nurtured so that they could soar`.

As soon as Mark walked through the revolving doors into the building, he was surrounded by the buzz of activity that comes with being productive. This humming was like a symphony that was made better by the sounds of phones ringing, computer keyboards clicking, and people talking in the background. It took him through the busy lobby and to the lift that was waiting for him. In the lift, he went up with a queue of professionals in suits or dresses. Each person was focused on his or her own goals, which over time became the organization's overall mission.

Under the gentle glow of artificial lighting, the office floor buzzed with activity, akin to a bustling beehive. His gaze fixed ahead, revealing an open-plan office adorned with desks that sprawled across a vast area, forming a bustling collection of busy cubicles. Employees conversed animatedly, their dedication and collaborative spirit evident in their focused demeanor.

For him, his dedicated workstation had transcended its utilitarian purpose; it had evolved into a personal sanctuary. Adorned with pictures of his family and cherished mementos, it reflected his values, accomplishments, and the essence of who he was. In this space, he found inspiration and motivation, making every day a journey of purpose and meaning.

He worked hard at his work, which he did with passion and a strong drive to be the best he could be while his computer hummed away.

His professionalism shone brightly as he handled the day's challenges in meetings, emails, and projects while also making connections and forming partnerships that helped the organisation as a whole succeed. At the end of the day, he carefully packed up his things, remembering what he had done the day before and giving quick glances and nods to his coworkers as he left.

The way he got home was similar to the way he got to work in the morning, but he used the time to think about what he had done at work and look forward to unwinding in walls that were familiar and full of comfort, welcoming him back into their peaceful atmosphere.

As soon as he stepped inside, he could feel the peace of his home. It was a safe place where he could find comfort each time they met, and it gave him a chance to relax before going on new adventures in the days to come.

His experience in the business world can be characterised as a tapestry of successes and failures that took place inside the hectic office environment. He entered the realm of possibilities with a heart that was heavy from the difficulties he had endured in the past. He was armed with an excellent education and a never-ending desire to be the best there is.

Him and his sister Jennifer had a hard time growing up without the love and direction of their parents. He didn't have any family to help him, but that didn't put out the fire in his heart. It made him want to rise above his situation and show that he could get through the hard things that life had thrown at him.

His rise in the company was nothing short of meteoric from the start. He began in a humble way, not standing out from the crowd. But he was different because he worked hard and never gave up. He moved up the corporate ladder through long hours of hard work and smart decisions that left his peers in awe of his determination.

His academic skills, which he honed while he was a university student, were the thing that moved him forward. He never stopped wanting to learn, and his intelligence was like a lighthouse that showed him the way. In classrooms and libraries, he ate up textbooks and learned more, making a lasting impression on both his teachers and classmates.

He was smart, but that wasn't what made him stand out. His humility and friendliness were what really made him stand out. Even though he worked hard to be successful, he stayed grounded and was kind and helpful to his coworkers. The name "the Sweet and the Scholar" became a nickname for him, which shows how well-rounded he was.

His time as a student scholar showed how hard he worked to be the best, but he also had to deal with problems along the way. Being an orphan and having to take care of his sister put a lot of weight on his shoulders. But that never stopped him from showing humility and kindness. In the worst of times, his Christian faith brought him comfort, and his belief in a higher purpose gave him strength.

As soon as Mark walked into the office, everyone was happy to see him. His coworkers admired not only how well he did at work, but also how much he cared about them as people. They saw him change as he rose above his classmates like a phoenix and became their leader. People admired and respected His rise to the top, and he became a symbol of the kind of success they hoped to have.

But success has a strange way of changing who a person is. His personality changed slowly but surely over time. Power and success gave him a high that made it hard for him to make good decisions. Every time he reached a new goal, his once-humble attitude started to change, and he became more and more cocky and proud.

He changed for many different reasons, all of which went back to his troubled past. As an orphan, he had scars from being left alone that showed up in his need for validation and recognition. As he moved up the ladder of success, his need to prove himself kept him from seeing the needs and struggles of other people.

The higher he went, the less he contributed. His once-strong sense of helping others started to fade as his own ambitions grew stronger. Once, he did a lot of kind things out of the goodness of his heart. Now, he's more focused on himself, which makes his interactions with others less pleasant.

His colleagues, who used to think very highly of him, were sad to see how he had changed. Warmth and friendship, which had been a big part of the office, were slowly replaced by a feeling of distance. His rise to power had left them without the compassion and understanding that had once brought them together.

Mark sat in the driver's seat of his car, lost in thought as he prepared to tackle the day ahead. Toronto's sprawling cityscape outside his window seemed to blur into endless possibilities, reminding him of why he had chosen to call this place home. He was driven by a deep thirst for success and a desire to make it big in an environment where ambition thrived. The magnetic pull of Toronto had been too strong to resist, with its vibrant energy and endless opportunities beckoning him towards a brighter future.

The lively streets and towering skyscrapers in Toronto mirrored Mark's internal landscape—a symbol revealing his insatiable hunger for success coupled with relentless determination. For inhabitants in this bustling city, excellence was non-negotiable; this inspired Mark to rise up against all challenges faced daily challenging environments across work situations. The moment he parked in front of work building; adrenaline rushed through him as he passionately gazed through the imposing structure before him; embracing all possible risks associated with making it big in such a competitive environment.

He pushed himself daily to achieve success while leaving traceable marks on Toronto's constantly changing terrain: enhancing these ideals inspired by sheer ambition driving unlimited possibilities awaiting discovery. At every moment within city walls, there loomed limitless potential to explore. With an unyielding conviction towards accomplishing all dreamt goals Mark fully comprehended the strain, yet walked into his office with a clear congeal mind.

 He knew he had to embark on another day of relentless pursuit towards achieving greatness through unwavering mental attitude, even when uncertainties abound. Ultimately, these critical internal musings forged ahead towards his journey – a driving force that propels him forward in making indelible marks at the highest level of success.

His ride up the corporate ladder was driven by an unquenchable desire for success. He worked long hours and missed out on time with his family. As he worked hard to reach his professional goals, the relationships he valued began to suffer because he didn't have time for them.

His absence and preoccupation made his once strong friendships weaken. His single-minded focus on climbing the corporate ladder slowly weakened the once strong bonds that had been built up over the years. The laughter, shared experiences, and heartfelt conversations that once made his life rich were now just faint memories that were hard to hear over the loud noise of his ambition.

Even romantic relationships couldn't stand up to the constant push for success. His proud heart, which was driven by an insatiable need for recognition and success, didn't leave much room for being vulnerable and getting close emotionally. He struggled to find a good balance between his personal life and his career goals, and he often forgot about the emotional needs of the people who wanted to love and support him.

His pride was hurt by the way he ignored and broke up with these people. Even though his successes in the business world made him feel good for a little while, deep down he felt a void, a hollow ache that couldn't be filled by professional praise alone. Pride was once what drove him forward, but now it weighed heavily on him because he knew he had given up important relationships to pursue it.

He couldn't stop thinking about what he had lost, even as he looked at all the things he had done and moved up the corporate ladder. In his pursuit of success, he had given up relationships that he once cared about. These relationships now haunted him, reminding him of the price he had paid.

When he thought about it, His proud heart longed for reconciliation, for a chance to fix the strained or broken bonds. He knew he had to rethink his priorities and find a way to balance his professional goals with the important relationships that gave his life meaning.

ONE

Co-workers were forced to communicate with one another in hushed whispers and stealthy glances due to the cramped conditions of the office. In a corner, a throng of people were huddled together, and the air around them was thick with rumours and speculation about what was going on. One of them was Nancy, a bubbly marketing manager with a flair for the dramatic. She was one of them. Another member of the team was James, an experienced sales executive who had a keen eye for office politics. Both of them were present. Mark's failed marriage was a constant topic of conversation between the two of them, as it was among the staff as a whole at the break room water cooler.

They made assumptions about what led to the relationship's demise, and their speculation was rife with accusations of narcissism and superiority complexes. When speaking to one another, they spoke in low tones, as if they were concerned that the other person might overhear them. rewrite best and infuse with dialogue conversation using the facts above to extend and increase the narrative

In the cramped office, co-workers communicated with hushed whispers and exchanged stealthy glances, careful not to draw attention to their conversations. In a corner, a group of people gathered, their huddled stance creating an atmosphere thick with rumors and speculation. Among them were Nancy, the vibrant marketing manager known for her dramatic flair, and James, the experienced sales executive with a keen eye for office politics.

Nancy leaned in, her voice barely above a whisper, "Have you heard about Mark's failed marriage?"

James nodded, his expression serious, "Yes, it seems to be the talk of the office. People can't help but speculate about what happened."

Nancy sighed, "It's a shame. I always thought they were a perfect couple."

James raised an eyebrow, "Really? I heard there were some issues beneath the surface."

Nancy looked intrigued, "Like what?"

"Well," James said, choosing his words carefully, "some people think it might have been related to Mark's tendencies of putting himself first."

Nancy shook her head, "I find that hard to believe. Mark has always been supportive of his team."

James shrugged, "Office dynamics can be complicated. You never really know what's going on behind closed doors."

Their conversation continued in low tones, as if they were afraid of being overheard. They delved deeper into the office gossip, exploring different angles and possible explanations for his failed marriage.

"I hope he is doing okay," Nancy said with genuine concern.

James nodded, "Agreed. It must be tough to go through such a difficult time in the spotlight of the office."

As they spoke, their shared curiosity about Mark's personal life brought them closer, creating a bond of understanding and empathy.

In another part of the office, Mark was oblivious to the hushed conversations about his marriage. He remained focused on his work, determined not to let the office gossip affect him. Instead, he found solace in his dedicated workstation, a place where he could stay grounded amidst the swirling rumors.

His reliable assistant, Maria, walked in just as they were getting deeper into the topic of conversation, and she joined in. The snitches were surprised by her presence for a moment, and when they looked at her, they did so with a mix of embarrassment and interest. Maria, a kind and level-headed person, walked up to them with a hint of sadness in her eyes.

"Maria, have you seen the changes that Mark has been going through recently?" Nancy questioned, her tone containing an equal measure of worry and interest in the subject matter.

Maria let out a long sigh as she scanned the group of people who had gathered in front of her with her eyes. "Yes, I have," was the hushed response from her. "It breaks my heart to observe the change that has taken place in him. However, let us not continue to linger on these pointless conversations any longer. We need to keep our attention on the tasks at hand."

James indicated his assent with a head nod while he was leaning against the wall. "Yes, you are correct, Maria. The accomplishments of our team ought to take priority over idle chatter. The change in Mark's demeanour, on the other hand, is difficult to ignore. He used to be such an admirable example to look up to."

Maria, the very definition of fidelity, gave him a gentle shake of the head. "I do comprehend your worries, but let us not forget that he is still in charge of our department. It is important that we stand behind him and encourage him as he works to rediscover the person that we admired. It is not for us to pass judgement or engage in idle chitchat."

Because they finally understood each other, they stopped talking, and the air took on a new tone. Everyone who was responsible for spreading rumours had a distinct physical presence that matched their personalities. Emily's fiery red hair and animated movements were two of the main reasons why people noticed her everywhere she went. She gave off a lively energy that made people pay attention to her. James's appearance, which was helped by the fact that he was tall and well-dressed, gave him an air of confidence that made people respect him.

Maria went back to her desk as the other members of the group went their separate ways, carrying the weight of the situation in her heart. The office was busy with activity, with the sound of clacking keyboards and ringing phones providing a background score for the chats that continued to buzz.

In the days that followed, Maria continued to be Mark's loyal ally, and her unflinching support shone like a ray of hope in the midst of a sea of scepticism. Even though his coworkers did not feel envious of his position, their level of concern increased with each passing day. As the excitement surrounding his impending promotion increased, he remains closer to the coveted position of being fourth in line for the role of Managing Director in the company.

They were worried that his growing pride had taken on a life of its own and had developed a force that was becoming increasingly difficult to control. Their fears were not motivated by envy; rather, they were motivated by the worry that his growing pride had taken on a life of its own. They longed for the man they had known in the past, one who was a respectful and motivational leader who lifted their spirits.

Despite the fact that the underlying unease remained, in the end, the subjects of their conversations eventually circled back around to the work that needed to be done. They continued to navigate the complexities of office life in the hopes that one day he would figure out how to get back to the person he used to be, and that this would inspire them to help him. Maria, ever the faithful confidant, remained a steadfast support for his boss despite the cacophony of ringing phones and bustling footsteps. She clung to the hope that the winds of change would carry them towards a brighter tomorrow.

❖

As raindrops tapped against the windowpanes. A sense of unrest filled the silent office where Mark Stevens worked as an executive in a powerful corporation. His once poised facade had crumbled under immense pressure from within. Leaving him drained and weary. He stared blearily at the computer screen before him but could not focus on any task at hand.

She noticed his recent strenuous efforts and the exhaustion etched on his face, which signaled that something was amiss. She gently inquired, "Mark, are you okay?"

He tried to brush off his irritation but couldn't hide his impatience, "I'm fine."

She, undeterred, kept probing, "Are you sure? Something seems off."

With a hint of frustration, he replied, "I said I'm fine. Don't worry about it."

Maria, concerned and persistent, attempted different approaches, "I'm here to help. You can talk to me if something's bothering you."

His responses remained guarded, leaving her unable to uncover the root of his troubles. Despite her best efforts, she couldn't break through his defenses, and the mystery of his recent behaviours baffled her.

She remembered a time when he was known as the epitome of professionalism and positivity in the office. Unfortunately. Over time. His persona appeared to change immensely until it became almost unrecognizable in contrast with the prior version, she so admired. It naturally concerned her to witness this cloudy air of superiority growing thickly and pushing others away instead of drawing them closer together. Her heart ached at the possibility that colleagues may no longer see him as a friendly face they could turn to for aid or guidance.

Despite putting forth her best effort filled with hope for change towards reminding him about how things used to be before and what he meant to so many people- it seemed that all the words she spoke were being ignored by him. For someone who had once been respectful. Kind-hearted, and understanding towards others around him- it was hard for Maria to comprehend how someone such as him could allow his own success and ambition erode these qualities within himself leaving nothing good behind but echoes of arrogance that served only in creating division amongst employees.

TWO

Exhaustion washed over him like a tidal wave as Maria exited the office. He sank back into his chair, visibly fatigued, his tired eyes seeking relief through gentle rubs. The long hours of work had taken their toll, leaving him drained and in need of rest.

Though Maria's concerns about his well-being were valid, his pride held him back from admitting the extent of his weariness. He had always been strong-willed, reluctant to show vulnerability even when facing the undeniable weight of exhaustion.

Outside, the weather seemed to mirror his inner turmoil. The atmosphere grew ominous, with lightning illuminating the side streets and torrents of heavy rain unleashed from turbulent thunderclouds. The wind howled fiercely through the town's streets, amplifying his feelings of unease and fear.

Despite the storm brewing both outside and within, he was determined to soldier on, bracing himself against the elements and his own limitations. Yet, deep down, he knew that he couldn't keep pushing himself without acknowledging the toll it was taking on him. It was time to confront his fatigue, find solace, and take the necessary steps towards self-care and restoration.

As he sat there, a gnawing feeling of needing to regain his strength and control washed over him. He felt lost, unsure of where to start or how to reclaim his sense of self. Just then, another flash of lightning streaked across the sky, accompanied by a loud clap of thunder. The sudden brightness made him jump, taken aback by the intensity of the storm.

Raindrops pelted the window, mimicking the chaos swirling within him. He recognized that his own pride, like a ravenous beast, had been consuming him, making him blind to his mistakes and hindering his ability to address them. With a heavy sigh, he acknowledged the growing burden of work, the errors he'd made due to his pride, and his uncertainty about how to mend the pieces that felt broken.

For a moment, he considered the irony of being frightened by a mere storm. But deep down, he knew that it was more than just the weather; it was the brewing tempest within himself that frightened him the most.

"This is just the beginning," he murmured to himself, gazing at the seemingly unending storm outside. Its persistent fury seemed to mirror the turmoil within his own soul, and he understood that he couldn't ignore it any longer.

Determined to catch up on his tasks, he arrived early at work the next morning. The office was abuzz with the familiar sounds of ringing phones and clacking keyboards as he made his way in. Striding past his coworkers' cubicles, he tried to maintain an air of confidence, reveling in his role as one of the company's top executives. However, he couldn't escape the disapproving glances his colleagues cast his way, which left him feeling a pang of guilt.

Later that day, a team-building activity was organized to foster better relationships and collaboration among the coworkers. He wasn't particularly enthusiastic about participating, but he found himself pulled into it nonetheless. He had never been fond of his coworkers, and those feelings simmered just beneath the surface.

Reluctantly, he joined the gathering, unable to ignore the tension that hung in the room. His past habit of talking down to and dismissing younger employees had left them wary around him. They exchanged knowing glances and whispered among themselves, a mixture of anxiety and curiosity evident in their voices.

The room brimmed with nervous energy and stifled amusement, creating an atmosphere of anticipation. His once imposing and intimidating presence now made his peers uneasy and cautious. They had witnessed his rude behavior and come to expect his preference for the company of those higher up on the corporate ladder.

In the midst of this team-building activity, Mark couldn't shake the feeling of unease that lingered within him. As he engaged with his coworkers, he knew that if he truly wanted to change and foster better relationships, he had to confront the consequences of his past actions and make a genuine effort to connect with his colleagues on a more equal and respectful level.

As he walked around the room, he overheard quiet conversations among his coworkers. They were talking with a mix of anger, doubt, and careful friendship. They shared stories that made fun of his ego and pointed out his weaknesses, showing that he seemed distant because of his pride, and he didn't have real connections with others in the office.

Amidst the charged atmosphere, an intriguing exchange began to unfold, reminiscent of a scene straight out of a captivating novel. The main characters of this tale were his coworkers, the very individuals whom his behavior had impacted. They regarded him with a mix of anxiety and determination, and the conversations continued with fervor.

"Did you see how he belittled Josh during the meeting?" whispered Sarah, her voice tinged with indignation.

Theodore chimed in, his expression a mix of skepticism and concern, "Yeah, it's a shame. He seems to love putting the younger team members down."

"They say he only hangs out with people in higher positions," Rebecca added cautiously, as if afraid of being overheard.

"Seems like he thrives on power plays, keeping himself distant from genuine connections," James said with a wry smile, "No wonder people are cautious around him."

The conversation continued, drawing in other listeners like an intriguing tale. Each person shared their perspective, shedding light on different aspects of Mark's personality. With each revelation, the interest of the listeners grew, eager to know the true character behind Mark's imposing exterior.

In the background, the team-building activity continued, providing a backdrop for the drama unfolding among the coworkers. Laughter and muffled cheers filled the space, but Mark stood at the periphery, silently observing a world he had chosen to distance himself from. The room buzzed with genuine bonding and new connections being forged, a stark contrast to the walls he had built around himself to keep people out.

The event organizers made an effort to break the ice and encourage cooperation and conversation. Mark's discomfort was palpable as he awkwardly engaged in small talk, yearning to be with people of his own status or higher. His attachment to the hierarchical structure made it difficult for him to connect with those he had previously ignored, creating a barrier between them.

After the event, he returned to his desk and delved into his work, poring over spreadsheets and reports to catch up. However, the continued disapproval from his coworkers only intensified his agitation. The feeling that they were talking about him behind his back gnawed at him, compelling him to confront the issue.

He walked right up to a group of his coworkers who were huddled together and whispering to each other. "What's happening?" Mark asked in a sharp, commanding voice. Not receiving any response from any of them, he walked up to them closer and said "Hey, um... I noticed some tension during the activity today. Did I do something wrong?"

A hushed silence fell over the group, and they gazed at him with a blend of shock and unease etched on their faces. Chiamaka, a Nigerian immigrant who had joined the company after completing her MBA program at the University of Toronto and had a razor-sharp intellect, broke the silence. "It's nothing, Mark. We were merely discussing work-related matters."

He made a face with his eyes. "It seemed like you were talking about me. Do you have something against me?"

She thought for a moment before softly speaking. "Mark, it's just that we care about you. You haven't stopped working for weeks, and we're worried that you're pushing yourself too hard."

His angry face turned red. "I don't need you to worry about me. I'm fine with how much I have to do."

Sophia, one of his coworkers, let out a soft sigh, her voice tinged with frustration. "It's not just that, to be honest, Mark. You often seem distant and dismissive towards us. It's difficult to connect with you."

His face flushed with embarrassment as he struggled to respond. "I... I didn't realize it affected you all that much."

Another coworker chimed in, "Well, it does. We're all here working together, and it would be nice if we could have a positive atmosphere."

Feeling defensive, he retorted, "Well, if it does, mind your damn business and do the work you came here to do! This is a company, not a social club!"

The group looked nervously at each other before breaking up. He was left to stew in the middle of the office. He sat down at his desk and shook his hands in anger. He seethed with anger as he discovered his coworkers gossiping about him. How could they not believe in him, especially when he was the top boss.

But as the day went on, he started to realise that his pride was making it hard for him to see the truth. He was so focused on getting ahead that he didn't pay attention to the needs of the people around him. When he looked out the window, the rain had stopped and the sun was starting to come out. He realised that he had been so focused on his work that he hadn't even noticed the weather.

He sighed and leaned back in his chair. He was thinking about his coworkers, his work, and how proud he was of himself. He knew he had to do something different, but he didn't know what to do. His life was very hard, but the sun shining on the city gave him a little bit of hope.

THREE

He had a big job in the company and was known for being smart and knowledgeable in his field. With a great education, he had learned a lot and gotten very good at what he did. His ability to consistently do great work had become a hallmark of his career. This gave him a reputation as a trustworthy and skilled professional.

He seemed so sure of himself that it was almost like he was bragging. He was confident in his skills and rarely asked his coworkers for advice or suggestions. He was sure that he knew more than anyone else about the projects at hand and often thought that other points of view were not important. He thought he was the best of the best, and his track record of success backed up this idea.

He was proud of the fact that he always did well, and he wasn't afraid to show off his accomplishments in front of people who were struggling. His habit of rubbing his successes in other people's faces, especially when they fell short, added to the idea that he was arrogant. His self-confidence was almost too high, which made it hard for his coworkers to ask him for advice or work with him.

He valued independence and being able to do things on his own because he wanted to be successful. He didn't trust what his peers had to say because he thought his own knowledge and expertise were much better. This way of thinking got in the way of working as a team and stopped the organisation from growing as a whole.

He was smart and had a good track record, which were both impressive. However, his way of working with others and his tendency to not care about what other people thought made for an environment of isolation and conflict. Even though he knew a lot, he didn't want to use the expertise and different points of view of his colleagues. This made it harder for the company to be innovative and work well together. He had always been proud of his business sense and ability to make good decisions. But his sense of pride had led him astray, and now he was about to make a huge mistake.

He was racing against the clock on a Friday afternoon to meet a deadline. He had to turn in a proposal by the end of the business day, and he was adamant that he would do it on time.

But as he read through the document, he found a small mistake. It was a small mistake, but if it wasn't fixed, it could have big effects. He didn't ask for help because he was too proud. Instead, he decided to fix the mistake on his own. He made a few quick changes to the file and then saved it without looking it over again. He didn't realise what a mistake he had made until the Monday after. The proposal was sent out with a very important mistake, and it was sent to the wrong people. The company was now dealing with a major setback, and he had to take full responsibility for it.

As he sat in his office by himself, he realised that his ego was the main reason he felt alone. He was so confident in himself that he couldn't bring himself to tell anyone that he was having trouble. But the weight of his ego was getting to be too much for him to handle.

He knew that he needed to do something to break out of his isolation, but he didn't know where to start. He couldn't breathe because of the weight of his ego, and he didn't know how to get rid of it.

The Company's Chief Finance Officer, Mr. Anderson, began a journey that would test not only his financial acumen but also his ability to navigate delicate conversations in the bustling hallways of Marks Company, where the symphony of business transactions echoed through the air. His proficiency in handling sensitive conversations and intricate financial situations would be put to the test on this adventure. This trip would put his abilities to handle complex conversations and complex financial situations to the test. His movements were deliberate and purposeful as he made his way to the office of Kenneth, the company's Chief Executive Officer; this was likely an indication of the gravity of the issue at hand.

Mr. Anderson had a distinguished appearance, with salt-and-pepper hair that was neatly combed and a pair of spectacles perched upon his nose. He was a man of salt-and-pepper hair. The charcoal grey hue of his suit exuded an air of professionalism, and the impeccable tailoring served to highlight the slim build he possessed. As he moved forward, he exuded an air of confidence that he had gleaned from his many years of experience as the keeper of the financial well-being of the company.

His meticulous nature was reflected in the fact that his office was located on the top floor of the building. The polished mahogany desk that was adorned with neatly stacked financial reports and the shelves that were lined with files that had been meticulously organised demonstrated his dedication to precision. His expertise and unwavering dedication to doing things the best way possible were attested to by the framed certificates that adorned the walls.

The journey from his office to the sanctum sanctorum of the CEO was one that could be interpreted both literally and symbolically. As he strode down the corridor, his mind was racing with thoughts of the impending revelation and the potential repercussions that could stem from it. With each advance, he moved closer to the centre of power and decision-making, which increased the magnitude of the responsibility that rested on his shoulders.

With nerves still tingling, he took a deep breath standing before the imposing office of the CEO. He rapped on the door with utmost care, and from within, a muffled acknowledgment echoed back. Steadying himself, he opened the door and stepped into the inner sanctum of the company's command.

The office of the CEO exuded elegance, adorned with cutting-edge artworks and floor-to-ceiling windows that showcased a breathtaking view of the cityscape. Kenneth, a towering figure himself, occupied a commanding position behind a magnificent Venetian red desk, emanating power and self-assurance. As Mr. Anderson entered, their eyes locked – the CEO's piercing blue gaze meeting the accountant's.

Mr. Anderson cleared his throat, "Good afternoon,Chief. I hope I'm not interrupting anything important."

Kenneth's firm voice resonated, "Not at all, Anderson. What brings you to my office today?"

He approached his desk while carrying a report that had been meticulously prepared. His determination was unwavering. The significance of the circumstance was illustrated by the heaviness of the document he was holding in his hands. He allowed himself a moment to gather his thoughts before continuing his conversation with him while maintaining eye contact with him.

"Sir," he began his speech, his tone steady and composed. "It is with great regret that I must inform you of a recent error made by the Marketing Manager, which has led to a significant financial loss for our company. The impact of his actions has reverberated through all our financial statements, resulting in substantial losses."

As the Chief processed the significance of the information, his expression hardened. The lines that were already present on his forehead became more pronounced, betraying his growing concern for the health of the company's finances. After there was a brief pause for silence, the man sat back in his chair and kept his attention focused on Mr. Anderson.

"Please enlighten me, Mr. Anderson; can you walk me through what happened?" He questioned, his voice indicating that he expected responses.

"Please explain what happened with Mark's misstep," he further requested, his voice steady but filled with curiosity.

He took a moment to gather his thoughts before responding, "Well, it all started when he made a series of risky financial decisions without thoroughly analyzing the potential outcomes. The consequences of those actions led to a significant financial loss for the company."

His eyes widened with concern, "How much are we talking about here?"

"It's a substantial amount, sir," he replied gravely. "The impact on our bottom line is quite severe."

He furrowed his brow, deep in thought, "I see. This is serious. We can't afford to take this lightly."

He nodded in agreement, "Exactly. We need to act swiftly and decisively to address the situation."

Chief paused, considering the best course of action, "I want a full analysis of what went wrong and a detailed plan on how we can recover from this setback."

Mr. Anderson affirmed, "I'll get right on it. We need to learn from this mistake and ensure it doesn't happen again."

As the conversation progressed, His initial shock transformed into resolute determination. He interjected with questions to gain a better understanding of the situation and to express his concerns.

"We can't let this financial loss define us," Chief asserted. "We must take responsibility and make the necessary changes to protect the future of the company."

Mr. Anderson agreed, "Absolutely, Sir. I'll present the findings and recommendations to the board, and together, we'll navigate through this challenging time."

In the end, an unwavering resolve filled the room. The reality of the financial loss was stark, but it also ignited a fire of determination within the CEO. He vowed to lead the company through this adversity, learning from the misstep and emerging stronger than ever.

However, the news of the company's financial setback spread like wildfire, and everyone was talking about him and his costly mistake. His was taken aback, fearing the repercussions of his actions. "I can't believe this happened. I hope Chief won't fire me for not catching this sooner," Maria, Mark assistant whispered to a colleague.

FOUR

The atmosphere within the company was tense, and discussions were buzzing with chatter. "Did you hear about Mark's blunder? It's causing a lot of trouble for the company," one employee said in hushed tones to another.

"Yeah, I heard Chief is furious with him. This is not good," the other replied with concern.

Overhearing the conversations, Mark's Assistant Maria couldn't help but feel worried for her boss. "I knew his pride could get in the way, but I never imagined it would cost the company so much," she confided to a close friend.

As the news continued to circulate, a renewed sense of vigilance permeated the ranks. Employees were determined to learn from this costly mistake and ensure it never happened again. "We need to be more diligent and thorough in our work. We can't let one person's arrogance bring us all down," remarked a senior staff member during a team meeting.

In the midst of this misfortune, the Chief Financial Officer stepped up to address the situation. "We need to assess the damage and come up with a recovery plan. We can't allow this setback to define us," he asserted during a company-wide gathering.

During this challenging time, the MD emotions were evident, and his anger at Mark's actions was palpable. "I trusted him with important decisions, and he let us down," he expressed during a meeting with the executive team.

Mark's Assistant, witnessing the gravity of the situation, felt a deep sense of responsibility. "I should have been more assertive in questioning his choices. I won't let this happen again," she vowed to herself, determined to learn from the ordeal.

Despite the shock and disappointment, the pursuit of excellence remained a guiding principle within the company. "We've faced challenges before, and we'll overcome this too. Together, we will rise stronger," the CEO declared, rallying his team to move forward.

❖

Ever since learning about the financial loss, conflicting emotions engulfed the CEO. Lost in a sea of deep thoughts, he pondered Mark's journey in the company. "Mark was exceptional, always working hard and making valuable contributions. He helped us reach new heights," he murmured to himself.

As he thought about recent events, worry clouded his heart. "It's painful to see Mark, who played a crucial role in our success, now facing blame for this setback," he admitted to his thoughts.

The CEO felt a mixture of sadness and concern about this new development. "The business world is unpredictable, and individual performance can have a huge impact," he reflected.

Feeling the weight of the situation, the CEO decided he needed to talk to Mark one-on-one. "I must understand what happened and find a fair solution," he determined.

Considering the gravity of the matter, he sought advice from the Board of Directors. "Their guidance will help me make the right decision," he thought.

The Chairman of the Board, Mr. Johnson, felt a heavy burden of responsibility following the financial loss Mark had caused after being briefed by the CEO. Determined to address the situation promptly, he swiftly requested the him to direct the company secretary to send out notices of an emergency board meeting along with all the necessary documents to the members of the board of directors.

As the clock struck the appointed hour, the directors of the company filed into the elegant boardroom, their faces reflecting a mixture of concern and determination. The long-polished table awaited their presence, and each high-backed leather chair bore the name of a distinguished board member. Mr. Johnson, the Chairman of the Board, took his seat at the head of the table, his presence commanding respect.

One by one, the directors found their places, exchanging nods of acknowledgment and greeting. The atmosphere was tense, with the weight of the impending discussion palpable. Mr. Johnson called the meeting to order, and all eyes turned to Kenneth, the CEO, as he began to brief the board on the grave situation caused by Mark, the Marketing Manager.

"Thank you, Mr. Chairman. Ladies and gentlemen, we are gathered here today to address a pressing matter concerning Mark's recent actions," Kenneth stated, projecting authority and composure. "These actions have resulted in a significant financial loss for the company, and we must address this head-on."

He directed their attention to the documents previously sent to each director, providing them with detailed reports and clear explanations of the financial impact caused by Mark's behavior. The board members listened attentively, their faces growing more serious as they absorbed the magnitude of the loss.

Sophia, a seasoned director known for her straightforward approach, was the first to speak up. "I think we need to take strong action. Mark's actions have not only caused financial losses but also affected team morale. I suggest we terminate his employment outright."

Mr. Patel, known for his pragmatic approach, chimed in, "While I understand the severity of the situation, perhaps a suspension with a chance for improvement might be a more balanced approach. We could suspend his promotion for three months and assign him a mentor to guide him during that period."

Maria, another director, leaned forward, "I agree with Mr. Patel. A suspension with a mentoring program could give Mark a chance to reflect on his actions and grow as a leader. But if after the suspension and mentoring, there is no improvement, I suggest termination as suggested by Sophia. However, for now, I don't support immediate termination. Remember, this young man has been an outstanding employee for years, helping the company not only grow but also become rich."

Sophia insisted, "But we can't afford to take any risks. Termination is the only way to show how serious we are about upholding our company's values."

Mr. Johnson, as the Chairman, skillfully moderated the differing perspectives, ensuring each director had an opportunity to express their views. "Let's put it to a vote then," he said. "All those in favor of immediate termination, raise your hands." A few hands went up. "And all those in favor of a three-month suspension with mentoring, raise your hands." The majority of hands supported the latter option.

"We have our decision," Chairman declared. "Mark will be suspended from his upcoming promotion for three months, during which time he will work closely with a mentor to address his behavior and improve as a leader. However, we also agree that if there's no significant improvement after the three months, we will reevaluate the situation, and termination may be considered."

Sophia grudgingly nodded, "Let's hope he takes this opportunity seriously."

"I hope so too," Mr. Patel added. "It's a chance for him to learn from his mistakes."

Mr. Johnson, with a sense of determination, concluded the meeting, "Let's ensure that our company's values are upheld, and we support him in his journey to become a better leader. We will reconvene in three months to review his progress."

As the meeting adjourned, the directors left the room, their footsteps echoing in the silence. The boardroom, with its long-polished table and high-backed leather chairs, bore witness to the gravity of the situation. The path forward was uncertain, but the hope for positive change lingered in the air. They were determined to see Mark's growth and the improvement of the company's overall environment.

After what seemed like forever, the rain finally stopped, and he could see the sun coming through his office windows. Even though the sun was shining brightly, he couldn't see how beautiful the day was. His ego made him feel empty and cut off from other people.

He suddenly realised that he couldn't hide behind his ego for the rest of his life as he sat at his desk and stared aimlessly at the computer screen. He knew that he had to deal with the facts of the situation he was in.

When his office phone suddenly rang, it jolted him out of his thoughts and back into the present. He answered the phone without first looking at who was calling.

"Hello?" he asked, but his voice sounded empty.

"Mark, can you come to my office? We need to talk. "The voice said without a corresponding greeting.

His heart dropped when he heard the news. He was aware of how important this was. It had been weeks since he tried to get away from his boss, and now he would have to deal with the consequences of what he had done.

FIVE

The offices were a hive of activity, filled with fast-paced movement that exuded productivity. The open-plan workstations, glass-walled meeting rooms, and shared spaces facilitated collaboration and idea-sharing. Being one of the most senior executives, Mark had his own office space in the building.

Amidst the busyness, three diligent office cleaners, John, Cynthia, and Angela, kept the place clean and organized. Angela, the youngest member of the team, brought a youthful energy to the group, working alongside the experienced John and Cynthia.

Early in the morning, the trio huddled together, taking a break from their duties to discuss their concerns. "Have you noticed how much Mark has changed?" John lamented, the wrinkles around his eyes deepening with experience.

Cynthia nodded, her eyes filled with curiosity and worry. "Yes, it's almost like he's a different person now. He used to be so polite and respectful to everyone, including us."

Angela tried to make sense of the situation, "It's hard to believe. You've known him for so long, and now he's acting this way?"

John sighed, his face reflecting sadness, "Indeed. Mark has come a long way in the company, but with success came arrogance. He no longer acknowledges our morning greetings."

Angela empathized with John's feelings, "That must be tough for you, considering how you've seen him grow over the years."

"It is," John admitted, memories flooding his mind. "I used to think of him like a son. Now, he won't even spare a moment to listen to me. I worry it might be his downfall."

Angela offered comfort, placing a hand on John's arm, "Maybe we can talk to him and remind him of who he used to be. Success shouldn't mean sacrificing humility and relationships."

Cynthia chimed in, smiling at Angela's kindness, "You're right, Angela. Let's not give up on him just yet. He might realize the importance of treating everyone with respect as time goes on."

Encouraged by their conversation, they returned to work with renewed determination. Though, their concern for Mark lingered, knowing that pride could have negative consequences. They hoped that, despite his current struggles, Mark would rediscover the values that defined him before.

As he approached his boss's office, the weight of his ego bore down on him heavily. He had always been confident, but now he felt like a failure.

The CEO, with a serious expression, awaited him inside his large and professional-looking office. Dressed in a well-fitted charcoal suit, the CEO exuded authority and self-confidence. The walls adorned with tasteful art and shelves filled with awards added to the aura of success in the room.

"Please have a seat," he gestured, his intense stare signaling the gravity of the conversation.

Feeling small in comparison to CEO grand desk, he sat down in a soft leather chair. The calm yet determined tone conveyed his disappointment and concern. "Mark, we must address the significant financial loss caused by your mistake and the growing tension among your colleagues," he explained.

His heart sank, guilt washing over him as he elaborated on the consequences of his actions.

"Our company's precision and responsibility are crucial for success. We must minimize such financial losses and ensure a harmonious work environment," he emphasized.

"I know you've been through a lot," he continued, softening his voice. "I value your contributions, but we must address this promptly and work together to improve."

He nodded, showing remorse and determination. He respected the CEO high standards and understood the importance of the company's financial health.

He urged him to reflect on the lessons from this experience, encouraging personal and professional growth. "We believe in your capabilities, but improvement is essential for long-term success," he emphasized.

Speaking further, his tone carrying concern, "the company's board of directors has resolved that your upcoming promotion, which you are due to receive along with a couple of other senior managers, will be put on hold under suspension for three months. During this period, a mentor will be assigned to you to ensure that you work on improving your work performance and interpersonal relationships, particularly within your department where you hold a leadership role.

I have personally decided to take on the role of your mentor because I believe in your potential and want to see you succeed. However, let me emphasize that if, after these three months, there is no discernible improvement, it may have implications beyond the delayed promotion, including your continued employment with the company.

The ball is in your court, and I sincerely hope you make the most of this opportunity for growth and improvement."

He felt a chill run down his spine upon hearing about the suspension of his promotion. "Three months... I understand," he replied, trying to steady his voice. "I take full responsibility for my mistake, and I am committed to making things right. I will work tirelessly to improve myself and my relationships with my colleagues."

His expression softened, showing a glimmer of hope. "That's the spirit, Mark. We all make mistakes, but it's how we learn from them and grow that truly matters. This setback can be a turning point for you, a chance to prove your resilience and dedication."

He nodded, feeling a renewed sense of purpose. "Thank you, sir, for giving me this opportunity to make amends. I won't let you down."

He offered a reassuring smile. "I believe in you, Mark. Just remember, challenges are part of growth, and I have faith that you'll rise to the occasion."

As he walked out of his office, he felt a mix of emotions – determination, fear, and hope. He knew the road ahead would be challenging, but he was ready to face it head-on. With the support of his boss and a renewed commitment to personal and professional growth, he was determined to turn his setback into a stepping stone towards becoming a better leader and a valued member of the company.

He thought that the sun shining brightly outside was a sign of a fresh start, so he took that to be the case. He realised that he couldn't let his pride keep him from reaching his goals any longer. It was time to face reality and do something that would make a difference.

SIX

The weight of his boss words hung in the air, making the rest of the day at the office feel sad. His mood was down and his heart was heavy with disappointment, so it was hard for him to get over what the CEO had said to him. He was no longer as happy as he usually was because a cloud of sadness had settled over him.

His sad expression stayed the same as the hours went by. Even though the office was busy, he felt like he was floating through a fog of self-reflection and thought. It became more and more obvious that he was not in the right frame of mind to keep working. He made a decision with a heavy sigh. Closing the office early seemed to be the only way to stop the overwhelming feelings that were going through his head.

He reached for the intercom and pushed the button. His voice had a tired sound to it. Maria, his trusted personal assistant, showed up at his office door almost right away with a worried look on her face. He showed her to come in without saying a word. She knew that the situation was serious and that now was not the time to ask questions or be nosy.

His voice was tired as he said, "Maria, please put all my calls on hold and cancel all my appointments for the rest of the day." She, who had worked closely with him for years, wanted to show her support or ask him why he had made the decision he had. Yet, when she looked into his eyes, she saw the clear signs of his withdrawal and his need for solitude in the face of trouble. She didn't say anything because she respected his need for space. Instead, she just nodded, leaving her offer of help hanging in the air.

As the bustling office carried on its usual business, he found himself in a cocoon of silence within his office. He couldn't shake off the weight of the conversation with his boss and the uncertain future that loomed ahead. He needed time to think, to gather his thoughts, and decide how to navigate the challenging road ahead.

As the day drew to a close, he felt a weariness that seemed to follow him home. The evening sky displayed hues of orange and pink, casting a sense of tranquility over the busy city. Yet, his mind was far from peaceful. The conversation with his boss kept replaying in his head like a broken record, and he couldn't shake off the feeling of impending loss that hung over him.

Lost in his thoughts, he drove through the familiar streets, seemingly unaware of the world around him. Memories of missed moments with his family and the sacrifices he had made for his career flooded his mind. In his pursuit of success, he realized he had lost sight of the important things in life.

As he drove on, he didn't notice the pedestrian crossing ahead and the traffic light turning red. Oblivious to his surroundings, he continued driving forward against the traffic rules, causing a wave of panic among pedestrians and other drivers. Horns honked, and people shouted, trying to warn him of the impending collision.

"Look out! What is he doing?!" a passerby screamed, pointing in Mark's direction.

"Oh my God! He's going to cause an accident!" another person yelled in fear.

As chaos erupted on the busy street, he finally snapped out of his thoughts and pulled over with a heavy heart. The flashing lights of a police car added an eerie glow to the scene, drawing the attention of more onlookers. A crowd quickly gathered, curious about what had transpired.

As Mark drove through the busy streets of Toronto, he couldn't shake the knot of unease in his stomach. Suddenly, his heart sank as he noticed the traffic light turning red ahead, but he was too close to stop in time and inadvertently ran the red light.

Moments later, Inspector Michael Ramirez, a stern and experienced Toronto police officer, pulled up behind Mark's vehicle in a police patrol SUV. Mark's heart pounded as Inspector Ramirez approached his car, his brows furrowed with concern.

"Good evening, sir," Inspector Ramirez said firmly and authoritatively. "I need to see your driver's license and vehicle registration, please."

Feeling nervous, he handed over the requested documents, and Inspector Ramirez glanced at the name on the driver's license.

As the officer checked his license and vehicle records, he discovered that he had a clean driving history without prior violations. His expression softened, revealing a mix of surprise and relief.

Returning to Mark's car, the police officer held the ticket book in his hand, signifying the consequences of his actions. "Sir, I must issue you a ticket for running a red light. Please ensure that you pay the fine within the specified timeframe," he stated firmly, adhering to his duty as an officer.

He accepted the ticket with a nod, feeling the weight of his mistake and the consequences that followed.

The crowd of onlookers slowly dispersed, but the incident left a lasting impact on their minds. "Did you see that? He could have caused a terrible accident!" one passerby remarked to another, their voices filled with shock.

"I know, right? Some people just don't pay attention while driving. It's scary!" the other replied, shaking their head in disbelief.

Meanwhile, he sat in his car, replaying the events in his mind. He knew he couldn't afford to make more mistakes, both on the road and in his professional life. The conversation with his boss echoed in his thoughts, and he realized that he had to make significant changes to become a better leader and a more responsible individual.

As the police officer finished issuing the ticket to him, he couldn't help but notice the emotional distress evident on Mark's face. Compassionately, he leaned in and said, "Are you alright, sir? I can see this has been a difficult day for you. Do you have someone you can call to accompany you home safely? It's crucial to ensure your well-being and the safety of others on the road."

Mark, appreciating the officer's concern, nodded and replied, "Thank you, Officer. I'll call my personal assistant. She can arrange for one of the company drivers to come and take my car. It's been quite a day, and I need to gather my thoughts."

He smiled reassuringly. "That's a good idea, sir. Take your time, and don't hesitate to reach out if you need any further assistance. We all have rough days, but it's important to handle them responsibly."

As he made the call, Maria arrived promptly with the company driver. "Hello Mark, I'm here to take your car, and I'll make sure you get home safely," she said with a supportive tone.

"Thank you, Maria. I appreciate your help," he replied, feeling grateful for the assistance during this challenging moment.

Officer Ramirez stepped forward and offered, "I'll escort you and make sure everything goes smoothly. Safety is a priority for us."

As the convoy navigated the streets, Mark found solace in the presence of the police officer, knowing that someone was looking out for him. During the ride, the officer offered some valuable advice, "Remember, it's crucial to address the challenges you're facing. Make sure to pay the fine within the given timeframe. Also, stay vigilant on the road to avoid any further incidents. Fortunately, your license was not suspended this time, but be mindful of the demerit points."

Mark nodded appreciatively, taking the advice to heart. "Thank you, Officer," he replied. "I truly appreciate your understanding and guidance."

The police officer smiled, "You're welcome. We all make mistakes, but it's essential to learn from them and be responsible on the road. Our main priority is to ensure the safety of everyone."

"I understand," he said, feeling a renewed sense of responsibility. "I'll make sure to be more careful in the future."

The officer continued, "That's the spirit. If you ever have any questions or concerns about traffic rules, don't hesitate to reach out or ask."

As the convoy continued its journey, he felt a sense of gratitude for the officer's advice and support. It was a valuable reminder to be mindful of his actions while driving and to prioritize the safety of himself and others on the road. With the officer's words in mind, he resolved to be a more responsible and vigilant driver in the future.

Finally arriving at his residence, the Officer bid farewell with a supportive smile. "Take care, Mr. Mark. Reflect on today's events and use them to grow. If you ever need assistance or have any questions, don't hesitate to contact us."

"Thank you for your help and understanding, Officer. I'll certainly keep that in mind," Mark replied, feeling a sense of gratitude for the officer's understanding and guidance.

As the Officer departed, he took a deep breath, feeling the weight of the day slowly lift off his shoulders. The ticket reminder remained, but now it served as a reminder of the lessons he needed to learn and the changes he needed to make.

Inside his home, his contemplated the events of the day. He knew he couldn't let this setback define him. It was time for introspection and personal growth. With renewed determination, he vowed to be more attentive on the road and in his role as a leader.

As the night settled in, his personal assistant, Maria, sat with him in the living room. She had been there throughout the ordeal and was concerned about his well-being. "Mark, I'm glad you decided not to drive home yourself. It was the right call to have the company driver take your car while you rode with the police officer," she said gently.

He nodded, appreciating her support. "I really needed some time to collect myself. I can't believe I let that happen," he replied, feeling a mix of regret and relief.

She placed a comforting hand on his shoulder. "Mistakes happen. What's important is how we learn from them and grow. Can you tell me what happened?"

He recounted the incident, explaining how he had inadvertently run a red light. He admitted, "I was distracted, lost in my thoughts about work, and I didn't even realize it until the officer pulled me over."

"It's understandable to get lost in thoughts, especially with all the responsibilities you carry," she empathized. "But it's essential to find a balance and be present, especially when driving."

"You're right, Maria. I need to be more mindful of my actions, both on the road and at work," he acknowledged. "The officer's advice and understanding really struck a chord with me."

She smiled reassuringly. "I'm glad to hear that. And I'm here to support you every step of the way. If there's anything you need or if you want to talk further about it, don't hesitate to reach out."

"Thank you, Maria. Your support means a lot to me," Mark said gratefully.

After spending some time discussing the incident, she bid him goodnight. "Take care. Remember, we all make mistakes, but it's how we handle them that matters."

As she left, he felt grateful for her presence and understanding. With her support and the guidance of the compassionate police officer, he felt more determined than ever to turn this experience into an opportunity for growth and positive change. He knew he had a strong support system in place and was ready to embrace the lessons from this day, becoming a more attentive and responsible driver and leader in the days to come.

SEVEN

He couldn't resist the allure of his favorite restaurant in the heart of Toronto. As he stepped inside, he was greeted by a delightful medley of mouthwatering scents. The menu offered a wide variety of dishes, each one showcasing the unique flavors from different parts of the world.

The restaurant offered a wide variety of dishes, ranging from fragrant and savoury Italian pasta dishes to hot and spicy Indian curries, to cater to the many different tastes of the people who lived in and visited Toronto. While Mark's eyes perused the menu, his mind was set on a specific dish that was guaranteed to sate his cravings: a mouthwatering plate of sushi that had been expertly prepared by Japanese chefs. Although his heart was set on a specific dish that always satisfied his cravings, his eyes scanned the menu.

As he savoured each delicate piece of sushi, his mind started to stray. Eventually, it came to consider the diverse array of cultures that flourished in Toronto. The city's diverse ethnic makeup was evident in the city's culinary scene, which was a reflection of the city's multicultural population. He was amazed at the variety of people he encountered on a daily basis, each of whom represented a different ethnic group and brought to the city their unique flavours, spices, and culinary traditions.

At a nearby table, a group of close friends could be heard laughing and swapping stories as they savoured the tangy flavours of Mexican tacos. A South Asian family was seated across from each other, enjoying a traditional South Asian dish called biryani. This multiethnic mosaic, which included people from all walks of life coming together to celebrate their heritage through the preparation of food, was so breathtakingly beautiful that he was powerless to help but be in awe of it.

His mind began to stray to all the exciting festivals and events that were crammed into the calendar of Toronto, showcasing the city's varied cultural celebrations like a rich tapestry. In a variety of ways, from the colourful parades of the Caribbean Carnival to the jubilant performances of Chinese New Year, the city embraced and celebrated its diverse population. His was thrilled to be able to partake in the many cultural traditions and sample the many ethnic foods without having to travel outside of his city.

He couldn't help but be grateful for the many excellent dining options Toronto had to offer. Because of a shared appreciation for culinary treats, the city's vibrant and friendly residents were able to feel a sense of community that cut across cultural barriers. With a newfound appreciation for Toronto's multiculturalism, he took his usual seat at the restaurant. He was looking forward to exploring the many different flavours and cultures that this multicultural city had to offer.

He continued to savour each bite of the sushi meal, his mind wandered again to the tantalizing flavors of African cuisine, particularly the renowned Jollof rice that reigns supreme in Nigeria. A chuckle escaped him as he reminisced about the friendly rivalry between Ghana and Nigeria, each vying for the title of the best Jollof rice. In fact, he had engaged in a light-hearted banter with his close friend Arinze, a Nigerian-Canadian who had joyfully introduced him to the richness of African culture and the culinary wonders it beheld.

His smile got bigger as he thought about his special friendship with Arinze, a friend from a different culture who had become his best friend. He was introduced to a whole new world of tastes and traditions by his lively personality and strong ties to his Nigerian roots. He had started on a fun journey of discovery because of his friendship with Arinze. He was led by his wealth of knowledge and love for his cultural roots.

He had taught him about the complexities of Nigerian food, especially how to make the perfect Jollof rice. He did this with a passion that matched his eloquence. His taste buds were hooked on this famous dish as soon as he took his first bite. It is known for its delicious mix of tomato sauce, perfectly cooked rice, and a mix of spices that smells great. With each shared meal and interesting conversation, he skillfully revealed the depth and complexity of Nigerian culinary traditions, painting a vivid picture of the tastes and techniques that made them so special.

He had learned a lot about Nigerian culture from his stories, including its many different ethnic groups, languages, and lively music and dance traditions. He had learned to appreciate the rich culture of Nigerian life through his vivid stories. He would never forget what he heard about the busy markets, the friendly people, and the important traditions that shaped their everyday lives.

He was happy that Arinze had shared his cooking skills with him by making him some delicious homemade Jollof rice. The experience had been nothing short of amazing, and every bite he took would stay with him forever. The delicious mix of flavours had teased his senses and made him salivate uncontrollably, which said a lot about how tasty Arinze's creation was.

The ongoing debate between Ghana and Nigeria over which nation produced the best jollof rice amused Mark.

He thought back to how Arinze had jokingly defended Nigeria's rendition, pointing out the special flavour combination and top-secret preparation methods that distinguished it from other renditions. He had the chance to sample the flavours of Ghanaian Jollof rice during his explorations of the world of food here in Toronto. Despite this, he preferred the friendly competition between the two nations and the fervour that surrounded the debate.

As he enjoyed his meal in the restaurant, a wave of gratitude came over him for the deep friendship he had made with him and the deep understanding of African and Nigerian culture he had gained through their friendship. It showed how important real connections are, how they can cross cultural boundaries and make everyone's lives better. He was lost in his own thoughts when a young woman with a warm smile and a name tag that said "Sakura" walked up to his table. This woke Mark up from his daydream.

"Is there anything else I can get for you, sir?" Sakura asked, her eyes full of genuine concern as she tried to figure out if he was enjoying his meal.

He looked up at her, smiled, and said, "Thanks for asking Sakura." The meal is delicious in every way. The flavours are wonderful, and it makes me think of all the great times I've had trying food from different cultures. Please tell the chef that I appreciate his work."

His enthusiastic answer made Sakura smile. "That's good to hear, sir. Our chef takes great pride in making meals that people will remember. If you need anything else, please let me know. Enjoy the rest of your meal!"

He nodded in appreciation. Sakura's genuine concern made him feel warm inside. "Thank you. I will do it for sure. The food here is not only delicious but also a celebration of different cultures, just like the friendships we make along the way.

She told him with a smile to enjoy the tastes that brought back so many memories and to keep being grateful for the connections that had changed the way he saw the world.

In that moment Mark made a mental note to call Arinze. Since they had last spoken, especially after he had returned to Nigeria with his family, it had been a while. Despite the physical distance between them and the hectic pace of their lives, which had temporarily hampered their ability to communicate, he was determined to reunite with his dear friend.

He mentally set a time and date for himself to contact him, feeling a sense of longing and anticipation. He understood that it was essential to maintain and strengthen their relationship despite the challenges that each of their lives presented. He was aware that their friendship was unaffected by the passage of time and the physical distance that separated them.

Having recently recommitted himself to working on their friendship, He made a solemn vow to himself that he would give making the call a higher priority. He understood the importance of their relationship and the joy that would be his when he heard Arinze's voice and shared in the many benefits of their friendship.

As he finished the mental note, he felt a rush of excitement and comfort at the same time. He was looking forward to catching up with him and rekindling the friendship that had grown between them throughout the course of their shared history.

After finishing his meal at the quiet restaurant, he sat back to relax a little so that food will digest and his mind drifted back to that fateful day at work when he had to confront the serious consequences of his actions. He couldn't shake the image of his boss's stern face and the heavy atmosphere of disappointment in the room. A wave of sadness washed over him as he delved deep into his thoughts, reflecting on his mistakes and their impact.

Lost in contemplation, he called the friendly waitress Sakura over to request the bill. Her gentle presence brought him back to the present moment. She approached his table with grace, placing the bill before him with a warm smile. "Here's your bill, sir. I hope you enjoyed your meal," she said with genuine kindness.

He smiled appreciatively at her thoughtful service. "Thank you, Sakura. The meal was delicious, and your service was excellent. Keep up the great work," he replied, leaving a generous tip to show his gratitude.

She thanked him with a nod, but his mind had returned to the thoughts that weighed heavily on him. He felt a mixture of emotions as he left the restaurant. The solitude allowed him the space to deeply contemplate the significant turning point in his life—the moment when the consequences of his actions prompted a profound change within him.

With each step he took, he engaged in a silent conversation with himself. "I've come to realize the importance of taking responsibility for my actions and the impact they have on others," he acknowledged.

In the midst of the bustling city, he found solace in his introspection. "Regret is a powerful teacher," he thought to himself. "I must learn from my mistakes and use this experience as a catalyst for personal growth and improvement."

As the city lights twinkled around him, he resolved to embrace change and demonstrate greater responsibility in all aspects of his life. The gravity of the consequences he faced had opened his eyes to the need for growth and self-awareness.

Upon reaching his car, he took a moment to pause and breathe deeply. "It's never too late to change," he murmured, reaffirming his commitment to a new path.

As he drove away from the restaurant, he felt a sense of hope and determination. He knew that facing the consequences of his actions had been a challenging but essential experience. It had sparked the beginning of a transformative journey—a journey toward personal growth, responsibility, and a brighter future.

EIGHT

Although he was aware that he needed to make amends, he was unsure of what to do next. He had lost the ability to look his coworkers in the eye and admit that he had made a mistake because he had spent so much time trying to hide behind his pride.

The following day, Mark found himself feeling restless at work, desperately seeking a distraction from the weight of his recent mistakes. He decided to take a break and wandered aimlessly around the office, hoping to clear his mind.

As he strolled, he caught fragments of a conversation between Maria and the new coworker, Agatha. Curiosity got the better of him, and he subtly moved closer to eavesdrop on their discussion.

Maria was known for her caring nature and willingness to help others. He could see Agatha appeared vulnerable, opening up about her frustrations with the new job. The challenges were overwhelming, and she felt lost.

Maria's voice was comforting as she said, "I understand, Agatha. Starting a new role can be tough, but trust me, you'll get the hang of it. Give yourself some time to learn and don't hesitate to ask for help."

Agatha sighed, "It's just that I feel so alone in this. No one seems to have the time or interest to guide me."

His heart sank further. He realized that he, too, had been one of those uninterested colleagues, too wrapped up in his own world to notice Agatha's struggles.

Maria smiled reassuringly, "Don't worry, Agatha. You're not alone in this. I'll be here for you, and I'm sure others will step up too. Let me introduce you to some more people who can offer guidance."

He felt a pang of guilt and regret. He had missed the opportunity to be there for her when she needed it the most. The realization that he had let his ego get in the way of being a supportive colleague weighed heavily on him.

As he continued to listen, another memory resurfaced. It was that specific incident involving Agatha seeking his help, and he had brushed her aside without a second thought. The memory was a harsh reminder of his lack of empathy and the consequences of his actions.

Determined to make amends, he waited for Maria and Agatha to finish their conversation before approaching her.

"Hey, Agatha," he began, trying to sound casual despite the nervousness in his voice. "I overheard your talk with Maria, and I wanted to apologize. I should have been more supportive when you approached me before."

She looked surprised but nodded, "I appreciate your honesty, Mark. It means a lot to me that you're willing to address this."

"I want to change," he continued earnestly. "I know I've been self-absorbed and not the best colleague, but I want to be different. If you ever need help or someone to talk to, I'll be here."

Her eyes softened, and she smiled, "Thank you, Mark. I'm glad you're trying to change."

From that day on, Mark actively made an effort to be more attentive and supportive of his colleagues. He engaged in conversations, offered assistance, and listened without judgment. Slowly, the office atmosphere shifted, and a sense of friendship grew among the team.

With time, he and Agatha developed a genuine friendship. They often discussed work challenges together, finding solutions as a team. The office became a place of collaboration and empathy, and other colleagues noticed the positive change

A wave of relief washed over him as he released the burden of guilt. Though he knew he had much to atone for, he remained determined to take the necessary steps towards redemption.

In the weeks that followed, he embraced his newfound commitment to being a better motivator for his coworkers. He actively sought opportunities to be a valuable team player, offering assistance and empathy to those in need. Listening attentively to their concerns, he made genuine efforts to understand and support them.

Admitting his own flaws, he acknowledged that pride occasionally got in his way, but he was learning to set it aside for the greater good. As he earnestly worked on himself, he began to witness the gradual return of trust from his colleagues.

The bright sunshine outside seemed to mirror the hope he felt within. He knew that the journey to redemption was far from over, yet he was filled with optimism. Each small step he took brought him closer to regaining his place as a respected and trusted member of the team.

.

NINE

He couldn't shake the realization that there was still a long way to go in repairing the fractured relationships with his coworkers, despite the progress he had made. As he sat at his desk, contemplating recent conversations and self-reflection, he understood that mastering humility was key to lasting change.

One particular conversation with John, the elderly cleaner whom he had always admired, kept replaying in his mind. He knew it was time to face the consequences of his actions and express regret to those he had hurt.

With newfound determination, he stood up from his chair and walked purposefully toward the area where the cleaners were working diligently. He felt a mix of anxiety and resolve as he approached John, knowing that he needed to make things right.

Clearing his throat, he addressed John with a tone of humility he hadn't expressed before. "Please give me a moment of your time, John, if you don't mind."

Turning around, John looked surprised to see Mark standing before him. As he nodded, the wrinkles on his face softened. "Mark, of course. What can I do for you?"

Taking a deep breath, he gathered his thoughts before speaking. "I apologize for the inconvenience, John. I have come to acknowledge the mistakes I made, particularly the arrogance and disregard I showed towards you and the other cleaners. It's not how I was raised, and it's not the person I want to be."

His face showed a mix of shock and cautious optimism as his eyes met Mark's. "Mark, I'm impressed by your honesty. Owning up to one's mistakes takes bravery. I must admit, I didn't expect this response from you."

Nodding, he conveyed his regret, and his words carried the weight of sincerity. "John, you are absolutely right. I let my successes cloud my judgment and forget the guiding principles that have always defined me. I failed to realize the importance of treating everyone with respect and empathy, regardless of their position in the organization."

Understanding flickered in his eyes, and his expression softened further. "We all make mistakes, Mark. It's admirable that you've come to this realization on your own. But what matters most now is the steps you take moving forward."

He nodded, a newfound determination in his voice. "John, I will honor my promise to you. I've decided to change. I want to mend the relationships I've neglected and restore the humility I've let slip away. I know it won't be easy, but I'm prepared to work hard to achieve my goals."

A teasing smile crept onto John's lips as he listened to his words. "Mark, I believe in second chances. If someone truly wants to change, they're capable of it. I'll give you the benefit of the doubt, but remember, change won't happen overnight."

He extended his hand to him, gratitude shining in his eyes. "John, I want to thank you for your kindness and capacity for forgiveness. I appreciate your wisdom and how you've guided me. I sincerely hope that, in time, I can regain your trust and build a stronger working relationship."

Taking his hand firmly, a glimmer of hope appeared in his eyes. "How about we start fresh? Let's work together to create a positive and respectful work environment for all employees in this company. And never forget, true leadership demands treating each person with the respect they deserve and embracing humility."

With that, they exchanged nods, signaling their commitment to a journey of growth and understanding. Mark felt a renewed sense of purpose as he stepped away. He was determined to mend relationships, apologize, and show his capacity for growth.

During his lunch break in the bustling business district, he sought solace in a nearby park that offered a welcome respite from the corporate environment. The park was a hidden oasis amidst the towering skyscrapers and busy streets, providing a refreshing escape for office workers like him. It was a serene Monday afternoon, and as he entered the park, the bustling sounds of the city gradually faded away, replaced by the gentle rustle of leaves and the melodious chirping of birds.

The well-maintained pathways led him through lush greenery, adorned with vibrant flowers that added splashes of color to the urban landscape. Benches were strategically placed under the shade of tall trees, offering spots for contemplation and relaxation. The park was alive with professionals seeking a moment of tranquility, eating their lunch, or engaged in quiet conversations with colleagues.

As he strolled along the winding paths, his troubled thoughts began to ease, and a sense of calm enveloped him. The park's serene ambiance provided the perfect atmosphere for introspection, away from the pressures and demands of the office. The weather was delightful, with the sun casting a warm glow, and the laughter of children playing in the nearby playground added to the soothing atmosphere.

Amidst the serenity, his attention was captivated by an elderly gentleman seated on a bench, gently feeding the birds that fluttered around him. The man's kind expression and gentle demeanor stood out in contrast to the fast-paced corporate world nearby. Drawn to this simple act of compassion, he felt an inexplicable attraction, prompting him to approach the elderly man.

As he neared the bench, the man looked up, his eyes meeting his with a serene warmth. A brief exchange of smiles followed, breaking the ice between them. He felt a connection to the man's peaceful presence, and he decided to take a seat on the adjacent bench.

He settled beside the old man on the weathered bench, the park embraced them with a sense of calm. The gentle rustling of leaves and distant hum of the city provided a soothing backdrop to their conversation. The sun dipped lower in the sky, casting a warm golden hue across the landscape.

The old man's eyes crinkled with a smile as he observed him. "You seem troubled, son. Is everything alright?" he inquired, his voice carrying the warmth of genuine concern.

Caught off guard by the perceptive observation, he hesitated momentarily before deciding to open up. "I have been facing difficulties lately. My pride has hindered my relationships with others, and I'm uncertain how to remedy it."

The man nodded, his expression contemplative. "Pride can be a perilous trait, my son. It blinds us to the needs of those around us and obstructs our personal growth."

He felt as if the man's words were meant for him, striking a chord deep within his being. "I now realize that, but I don't know how to change my ways."

The old man smiled at him kindly, radiating a sense of tranquility and wisdom. "Humility is the solution, my son. You must be willing to acknowledge your mistakes and seek assistance when necessary. It is not an easy path, but it is a worthwhile one."

The park, a sanctuary of serenity amidst the bustling city, had always been his refuge. Towering trees provided a canopy of shade, offering solace from the afternoon sun. Bees buzzed busily from flower to flower, and butterflies danced in the gentle breeze. The faint hum of cicadas created a symphony of nature's melody.

As the old man began to speak again, his voice carried the weight of experience and lessons learned. He shared a tale that seemed to weave itself into the very fabric of the park. It was an embroidery of vibrant threads, featuring a young man who bore a striking resemblance to him. This young man, driven by ambition and an unwavering desire for success, had allowed his pride to consume him.

He found himself captivated, drawn deeper into the story with each word. The park seemed to hold its breath, as if nature itself were attuned to the old man's tale.

The old man's voice took on a storyteller's cadence as he continued, "Once, there was a young man much like you, filled with aspirations and dreams. He believed that pride was a virtue, a necessary fuel to propel him forward in the corporate world. But as he climbed the ladder of success, his unchecked pride cast a dark shadow over his relationships and blinded him to the true essence of life."

He listened intently, feeling a connection to the young man's journey. He saw glimpses of his own life reflected in the story, recognizing the parallels between his path and that of the young man.

With a touch of nostalgia, the old man painted vivid scenes of the young man's interactions with colleagues and loved ones. "He was brilliant in his work, achieving accolades and recognition. But in his pursuit of individual success, he lost sight of the people around him. His pride led him to dismiss the needs and concerns of others, and he became isolated in his achievements."

As the tale unfolded, his heart grew heavy with the weight of realization. The old man's storytelling skill kept him captivated, and the park around them seemed to transform into a stage for the young man's life journey.

The old man's voice softened with empathy, "The young man found himself surrounded by admirers who applauded his triumphs but lacked true connections. He felt an emptiness, a loneliness that achievements could not fill. He yearned for meaningful relationships, but his pride had built walls around him."

His expression mirrored the emotions stirred within him. The realization of the consequences of unchecked pride resonated deeply.

"However," the old man continued, "there came a moment of awakening for the young man. A moment when he saw the emptiness in his heart and the toll his pride had taken on his life. It was a turning point that filled him with a yearning for change, a desire to rediscover humility and compassion."

As the tale neared its pivotal moment, the park seemed to hold its breath, anticipating the young man's transformation.

"In that moment of clarity," the old man said, his eyes glimmering with wisdom, "the young man set out on a journey of self-discovery. He sought guidance from wise mentors, opened his heart to honest conversations, and learned the art of empathy. It wasn't an easy path, but it was a transformative one."

He felt a surge of hope within him, inspired by the young man's determination to change.

The old man's voice grew somber as he continued, "But sadly, the young man's realization came too late. His unchecked pride had already caused irreparable damage. He had lost the trust of his colleagues and the respect of his loved ones."

The park seemed to echo with the weight of the young man's mistakes, and Mark's heart sank as he heard of the tragic consequences of pride.

The old man concluded with a tinge of sorrow, "He lost everything he held dear, including his wife and children. His obsession with success left him isolated and broken."

Tears welled up in his eyes as he absorbed the gravity of the young man's story. The park, once a sanctuary of serenity, now held a cautionary tale of the perils of unchecked pride.

As he sat in silence, the old man placed a comforting hand on his shoulder. "Learn from this young man's mistakes, my son. Embrace humility, mend your relationships, and cherish the love of those who truly care for you. The path to redemption is never easy, but it is possible."

With a renewed sense of purpose, he rose from the bench, ready to bid farewell and carry the invaluable lessons with him. However, just as he was about to leave, the old man gently touched his arm, his eyes filled with a mix of sadness and wisdom.

"Wait, young man," the old man's voice quivered with a tinge of melancholy. "I have one more truth to share with you."

Intrigued, he hesitated, his footsteps faltering. He turned to face the old man; his heart heavy with anticipation. "Please, go on," he softly urged.

A heavy sigh escaped the old man's lips, his gaze fixed on some distant memory. His demeanor exuded a sense of resignation and a lingering aura of loneliness. His face, etched with lines of experience, bore the weight of countless untold stories.

"You see, young man," the old man began, his voice filled with quiet sorrow, "I am the man in the story. The consequences of my pride have followed me through the years, leaving me with a life ravaged by loss and regret."

His eyes widened, disbelief etching itself onto his face. He studied the old man, suddenly seeing him with new eyes, recognizing the subtle similarities in their journeys.

"You lost your children, your wife, and so much more," He murmured, his voice filled with empathy and a hint of sorrow.

A nod of affirmation came from the old man, his eyes glistening with unshed tears. "Yes, my friend. The consequences of my pride were far-reaching, seeping into every corner of my existence. I stand before you now as a lonely old man, burdened by the weight of my choices."

John, who had been quietly observing the conversation from a nearby bench, listened intently to the revelation. His face displayed a mix of surprise and understanding, his wrinkled features contorting with empathy.

Mark's heart sank, a sense of shared grief washing over him. He reached out and placed a hand on the old man's frail shoulder, a gesture of compassion and solidarity. "I'm so sorry for all you've endured. Your story has touched me deeply, and I will carry its lessons with me."

The old man offered a faint smile, the creases of his face deepening with bittersweet appreciation. "It warms my heart to know that my story has found resonance within you. Learn from my mistakes, young man, and make amends while there is still time."

The park seemed to hold its breath as the weight of the old man's words settled in the air. The sun, hidden behind a veil of clouds, cast a muted glow upon the scene, accentuating the poignancy of the moment.

Mark, now acutely aware of the consequences of unchecked pride, vowed to honor the old man's story by living a life of humility and compassion. He promised himself that he would mend the broken relationships, seek forgiveness, and forge genuine connections before it was too late.

With a heartfelt nod of gratitude and understanding, Mark bid farewell to the old man, his steps lighter but his heart burdened with the weight of the lesson learned. As he walked away, the old man remained seated on the bench, a solitary figure bathed in the fading sunlight, forever marked by the consequences of his pride.

John, having witnessed the profound exchange, remained rooted to his spot, his eyes fixed on the old man. He pondered the fleeting nature of pride and the enduring impact it had on the human soul.

It was a moment that etched itself into John's memory, a stark reminder of the fragility of life and the importance of genuine human connection. He approached the old man, a sense of empathy radiating from his weathered face.

"Sir, I couldn't help but overhear your conversation with Mark," John began, his voice laced with a mixture of compassion and curiosity. "Your story touched me deeply, and I want you to know that you're not alone."

The old man turned his gaze towards John, his eyes reflecting a lifetime of pain and regret. He listened intently, finding solace in John's empathetic words.

"You see, I've witnessed firsthand the impact of pride on people's lives," he continued, his voice growing stronger with each word. "And it breaks my heart to see the toll it has taken on you. But I believe in redemption, in the power of forgiveness and second chances."

A flicker of hope danced in the old man's eyes, a glimmer of possibility amidst the sea of regrets. He nodded, his expression a mix of gratitude and weariness.

"I may not be able to change the past," his voice filled with determination, "but I can be a source of support and understanding. Together, we can navigate the path of healing and self-forgiveness."

The old man's weathered hand reached out, gripping John's with surprising strength. It was a silent agreement, a shared commitment to embark on a journey towards reconciliation and inner peace.

As Mark walked away, a renewed sense of purpose burning within him, he cast a final glance back at the old man and John. He saw a flicker of hope amidst the shadows of regret, and it gave him reassurance that change was possible.

In that park, where stories intersected and lessons were learned, three souls stood connected by the profound impact of pride. Mark, the young man who had been awakened to the consequences of his actions, resolved to mend the fractured relationships in his life. The old man, burdened by the weight of his past, found solace in the compassion of a stranger. And John, the wise observer, vowed to be a guiding light in their journeys towards redemption.

The park, once a backdrop of solitude, now bore witness to the stirring of transformation. And as the sun dipped below the horizon, painting the sky with hues of gold and purple, a glimmer of hope illuminated the hearts of those who dared to confront their own pride and seek a path of healing.

In the twilight of that fateful day, the old man's story continued to echo in the minds of those who had listened. Its impact would ripple through their lives, reminding them of the profound lessons learned about the cost of pride, the power of humility, and the enduring strength of forgiveness.

TEN

He had come a long way in becoming a humble person, but the weight of his past mistakes still weighed heavily on him. He was still conscious of how his pride had hurt others, and he was unable to shake the overwhelming sense of regret.

During a pleasant Saturday morning stroll through the busy city streets of Toronto, he inadvertently ran into Alex, a childhood friend. The warmth of their friendship persisted even though time had separated them.

Mark, hey! How are you doing? he asked with a sincere smile on his face.

He felt a wave of guilt come over him as he looked at Alex. His mind was filled with memories of how he had consistently put his own needs ahead of theirs, letting his pride get in the way of their friendship.

He replied, visibly uneasy, "I've been doing okay."

At that exact moment, his heart was filled with a strong mix of regret and longing. He thought back to a time when he and Rachel, Alex's sister, had a touching conversation at a small café. The room was lit with a soft glow, making it a cosy place for them to talk.

During that deep conversation, she told him about a personal problem that had been bothering her for a long time. Her eyes sparkled with tears she hadn't yet shed. She was silently pleading for help and understanding. It was a moment of weakness that called for understanding and kindness.

But his pride, which had been a strong enemy for a long time, came back to haunt them and put a cloud over their relationship. Because his own ego was so big, he couldn't see how much she hurt. Instead of offering comfort and solace, his response was full of insults that made her struggle seem less important. She felt like she wasn't being heard or cared about because he couldn't really understand how she felt.

He felt bad when he thought about what he had done. He realised how insensitive he had been and how his selfishness had hurt other people. The weight of his misplaced pride had hurt the relationship he had with her and left him with deep wounds. With a heavy heart, he wished he could go back in time to show her the compassion and understanding she needed and deserved so badly. He longed for the chance to fix their friendship and make a place where empathy and openness could grow.

At that crucial time, she felt rejected and abandoned as his pride pierced her heart. The trust that once served as the foundation of their friendship broke, and its ruins were dispersed by the wind. The unbreakable connection, which was based on unwavering trust and mutual support, was now on shaky ground.

His pride weighed heavily on her, leaving her with deep wounds that persisted for a long time after their encounter. The hurt of his dismissal left an indelible mark on her mind, destroying the haven of their shared experiences. His inability to put his ego aside and show Rachel the compassion she so desperately needed widened the gap between them.

She withdrew into a world of self-preservation in response to this broken trust, protecting her heart from additional hurt. As his pride loomed between them, the once-warm and personal connection they shared gave way to an icy distance.

Alex looked at him with a serious expression. "Mark, I need to discuss something with you. Do you remember Rachel, my sister?

He nodded while feeling a knot in his stomach. He was prepared for this discussion.

Alex continued, a look of disappointment etched across his face, "she told me about what happened between you two. "Your pride got in the way and hurt her. I thought you were above that, man.

After getting punched in the stomach, he couldn't have felt any worse. Even though he knew what would happen because of what he did, hearing it from him made it seem even more real. "Alex, I understand. He said, barely raising his voice above a whisper, "I'm so sorry.

As he looked at him, his expression grew softer. "You have my trust, Mark. However, a simple apology is insufficient. You should apologise. You can't just assume everything will be fine. You must demonstrate your progress.

"Again, there's something else I need to tell you," Alex said, his voice tinged with concern. "She lost her job, and is also going through a tough time in her personal life."

Mark's eyes widened in surprise, "Oh no, what's been happening?"

Alex hesitated before continuing, "Her marriage has been falling apart. She and her husband have been going through a rough patch, and it's taking a toll on her emotionally."

Worry creased Mark's brow, "I had no idea she was going through all of this. She must be feeling so overwhelmed."

"Yes, she is," he replied somberly. "And she really could use a good friend right now. I know it's been a while, but reaching out to her would mean a lot."

Feeling a deep sense of responsibility, he nodded solemnly, "You're right, Alex. I shouldn't have let work consume me to the point of neglecting my friends. I'll call her immediately and let her know I'm here for her."

He smiled appreciatively, "I'm glad to hear that, Mark. I know it'll mean the world to her to hear from you."

He was thinking a lot about how much his pride had cost him as he said goodbye to Alex. He had damaged his reputation, lost friends, and hurt people he cared about. Mark decided to start a path of self-improvement after realising that he must continue to work on developing humility in order to prevent the dangers of pride in the future.

ELEVEN

He took a deep breath as he dialed her number, his fingers trembling slightly with nervous anticipation. After a few rings, she answered the phone, her voice warm and familiar.

"Hey, Rachel, it's Mark," he said, his heart beating a little faster with nervousness. "Long time no talk. How have you been?"

On the other end of the line, Rachel sounded pleasantly surprised, "Mark! It's really nice to hear from you. I've been doing well, thanks. How about you?"

Mark couldn't help but smile, feeling more at ease with her friendly response. "I've been good too, just busy with work and all. Hey, I was wondering if you'd like to meet up for coffee sometime. I'd really love to catch up and talk."

There was a brief pause before Rachel replied, "Sure, Mark. I'd like that. It's been a while since we've seen each other."

Relief washed over him as he responded, "Great! How about we meet at that cute café downtown, the one with the warm colors and comforting smell? Tomorrow afternoon works for me. What about you?"

She agreed, saying, "Tomorrow sounds perfect. See you there at 3 p.m."

"Perfect. 3 pm it is," Mark confirmed, a smile tugging at the corners of his lips.

On a crisp autumn afternoon, the next day, he walked into the quaint café with a sense of anticipation. The café exuded a cozy charm, adorned with warm wooden furnishings and soft, dim lighting that created an inviting atmosphere. The aroma of freshly brewed coffee enveloped the air, mingling with the sweet scent of freshly baked pastries, enticing the patrons inside.

As he stepped in, he noticed the bustling crowd of people engaged in animated conversations. Some were huddled over laptops, typing away with focused expressions, while others engaged in laughter and companionship with friends. The gentle hum of chatter blended with the soothing background music, creating a symphony of ambiance.

He wore a simple yet sophisticated outfit, donning a navy-blue sweater over a crisp white shirt and dark jeans. He looked both elegant and approachable, the kind of attire that suited the cozy café setting.

His heart raced as he found the perfect spot near the window, offering a view of the golden-hued leaves gently swaying in the autumn breeze. Nervously, he adjusted the position of his chair, facing the entrance, waiting eagerly for Rachel's arrival.

And then she walked in, a vision of grace and resilience. her dark hair was styled in a loose ponytail, framing her face delicately. She wore a soft, emerald green dress that complemented her radiant smile. The sunlight cascaded over her like a warm embrace, casting a natural glow on her features.

He stood up as she approached, greeting her with a genuine smile. "Rachel, it's so good to see you," he said warmly.

She returned the smile, her eyes softening as she spoke, "Likewise, Mark. Thank you for inviting me."

He gestured towards the cozy corner table he had chosen. "Shall we sit over there? It's a great spot with a lovely view," he said, holding out the chair for her in a gentlemanly manner.

Her cheeks flushed slightly, appreciating the gesture, and she gracefully took her seat. "Thank you," she replied, her demeanor a mix of curiosity and guardedness.

As they settled into their seats, the friendly barista approached to take their orders. He chose a soothing chamomile tea, while she opted for a comforting cappuccino with a sprinkle of cinnamon on top.

The café ambiance seemed to mirror their feelings, calming and warm, yet with a hint of tension. He took a deep breath and began the conversation with genuine concern in his voice.

"I spoke with Alex recently, and he told me about what you've been going through," he said gently.

Her expression softened as she nodded, "Yes, it's been a challenging time, losing my job and all."

"I had no idea," he admitted, his voice tinged with regret. "I wish I had been there for you when you needed someone. I'm truly sorry for not being a better friend."

She studied his face, searching for sincerity in his words. "It did hurt that you didn't respond to my attempts to get in touch," she confessed.

"I understand," he replied earnestly. "And I'm here now to make it right. I've been doing some serious self-reflection lately, and I realize how much my pride has affected my relationships. I want to change and be a better friend."

She observed him carefully, seeing a glimmer of hope in his eyes that he had indeed changed. She decided to give him a chance, but her guard was still up.

"It's going to take more than just words, Mark," she said firmly. "I need to see real changes in your behavior."

He nodded, determined to prove himself. "I'm willing to do whatever it takes. I value our friendship, and I want to be there for you."

As the conversation continued, he couldn't help but recall what Alex had confided in him about Rachel's marriage troubles. He hesitated, unsure if he should broach the sensitive topic.

"You know, Rachel," he began cautiously, "Alex also mentioned that you are having some trouble in your marriage. He's worried about you and what you're going through."

Her demeanor shifted slightly, and she looked uneasy. "Oh, really? I didn't think it was that obvious."

He sensed that she might be denying the extent of the issues. "You don't have to hide anything from me, you know," he urged gently. "We've been friends for so long, and I want to be here for you through thick and thin."

She sighed, her countenance betraying that there was more to the story than she was willing to reveal at first. "Alright, maybe I haven't been entirely honest," she admitted hesitantly. "Things haven't been going well with my husband. We've been having arguments and drifting apart."

He listened attentively, providing a comforting presence. "I'm here for you, Rachel," he assured her. "You can always talk to me about anything. We'll figure this out together."

As their conversation flowed, their body language eased, and the café seemed to cocoon them in a bubble of understanding and vulnerability. They laughed together, reminiscing about their college days, and shared their experiences of love, loss, and growth over the years.

The passing time seemed inconsequential as they connected, rediscovering the bond they once cherished. The café, with its comforting atmosphere, witnessed their healing and transformation, just like the falling leaves outside hinted at the changing seasons of their friendship.

By the time they said their goodbyes, she felt a glimmer of hope that their friendship could indeed be rekindled. He, on the other hand, felt a renewed sense of purpose, knowing that the journey of rebuilding their bond had just begun.

As the sun dipped below the horizon, casting a warm golden glow on the café's window, they parted ways, knowing that they were both willing to put in the effort to make their friendship stronger than ever before. And in that cozy café, amidst the gentle sounds of laughter and the aroma of coffee, they took a step towards healing and a future filled with warmth and understanding.

In the days that followed, he made a conscious effort to be there for her, checking in on her regularly and offering a helping hand whenever she needed it. Their friendship grew stronger, and they both realized the importance of being honest and vulnerable with each other.

Through their conversations and support, she found the courage to confront the issues in her marriage and work towards resolving them. And as for him, he learned the value of humility and empathy, understanding that being a good friend meant being there not just in the good times, but also during the difficult ones.

Their friendship, now rekindled with newfound trust and sincerity, blossomed like never before. And in the face of life's challenges, they knew they could rely on each other, just as true friends should.

TWELVE

He had made a lot of progress in mending his broken relationships, but there was still one person he hadn't talked to yet: Sarah, his ex-wife. The end of their marriage had caused a lot of pain and regret, and his stubborn pride had caused damage that couldn't be fixed. Even though they had been divorced for a while, his guilt still weighed on him and reminded him of how much pain he had caused her.

In the back of his mind, he had a bittersweet flashback that took him back to the beginning of their once-cute love story. They were college sweethearts, two young people starting out on a journey of friendship and dreams together. It was a happy accident that their eyes met in a crowded room on a warm summer evening. At that very moment, there was an unmistakable spark that drew them together with a magnetic force.

Their love grew like a soft flower, full of life and promise of a future together. They started dating quickly because they had the same hopes and dreams and a strong bond. During their college years, they laughed, talked late into the night, and stole kisses under a moonlit sky. Together, they built a relationship based on trust and common goals, and they believed that their love could get them through anything.

But as time went on, it became clear that their relationship was not very strong. His sneaky pride crept into their once-happy relationship like an unwelcome guest. Its presence cast a shadow over their relationship and weakened their ability to understand and care for each other. As his pride crushed their love, their relationship ended. His pride had a destructive effect on their love. Their dreams fell apart, and they both feel very sad about it.

The clear memory of that lovely summer evening came back to him, and it reminded him of all the possibilities they had once had. His heart hurt when he realised that he was to blame for the painful breakup, which had changed the course of their lives for good. As he thought about the times they had spent together, he felt a strong mix of regret, longing, and a tiny bit of hope.

His determination grew with each passing day. He was driven by a strong desire to find redemption and closure. He longed for a chance to talk to her, sincerely apologise for the pain he had caused, and say how sorry he was for the lost moments and broken dreams. It was a hard thing to do, but he knew that facing the consequences of his actions was the only way to get better.

As he set out on this daring journey of reconciliation, he held on to the hope that even though love had been hurt, it could still find a way to heal.

In the beginning, their relationship was like a beautiful embroidery, full of trust, support, and shared goals. He enjoyed all the love and admiration he got, and his pride was boosted by how happy they were when they were together. Their love shone like a lighthouse, giving them hope as they walked together.

But as time went on, the seeds of his pride started to grow, destroying the foundation they had worked so hard to build. His big ego made him put his own wants and goals ahead of their shared goals, which made the gap between them grow wider and wider. Because of his pride, he didn't care about her ideas or goals and didn't think she was worth much.

As the distance between them grew, their once-close conversations became tense and full of anger. His pride made him always want to be right, which left little room for understanding or compromise. Their love, which used to be strong and unbreakable, slowly died under the weight of his ego, which killed the tenderness that had once made them a couple.

She was stuck in a marriage she didn't like, so she turned to other people for comfort and companionship. His pride and emotional neglect put her under a lot of stress, and she turned to cheating to find the emotional fulfilment she couldn't find in their crumbling relationship.

When he found out that she had lied, it broke what little trust they had left. They couldn't get over the deep hurts that their actions had caused, so they had to make the heartbreaking decision to go their separate ways.

She fought hard to get custody of their two kids. The pain she had been through had left her with deep scars. He, on the other hand, was too focused on his pride and ambition to care about playing a meaningful role in his children's lives. He told his lawyer not to ask for either full custody or joint custody. Instead, he chose to fulfil his parental duties only by paying child support. Because he was so dedicated to his career, he made this choice, which left him with little time and involvement in raising his children. He thought that taking care of his kids or spending time with them would get in the way of his ambition. He chose to stay away from the day-to-day responsibilities of being a parent instead.

The divorce was the bitter end of their broken dreams. It was a painful realisation of the irreparable damage that his pride and their emotional distance had caused. The weight of their failed marriage hung over their lives and the lives of their kids for a long time.

In his deepest thoughts, He was haunted by the effects of his pride, realising that he was the main reason why their once-sweet marriage broke up. The memory of his mistakes was a powerful reminder of how important it is to be humble, have empathy, and take an active role in a relationship if you want it to be loving and close.

After much contemplation, Mark finally found the courage to reach out to his ex-wife. His hands trembled slightly as he dialed her number, each digit filled with memories of the past. The phone rang, and with every passing second, his heart pounded louder in his chest. When she answered, his voice was a potent blend of fear and longing, "Hey... it's me."

There was a pause on the other end, and he could sense the weight of their history in the silence. Finally, her hesitant "yes" broke the stillness, and a whirlwind of emotions engulfed him.

"Would you be willing to meet in person?" Mark asked, his voice filled with hope.

There was a pause on the other end, and he could sense the weight of their history in the silence. Finally, she asked softly, "Why do you want to meet?"

"It's important, Sarah," he replied, his voice earnest. "There are things I need to say, things that I think we should talk about in person. I promise I'll explain everything when we meet."

She hesitated for a moment before finally saying, "Alright, I'll meet you."

Relief washed over him as he heard her agreement. They decided to meet at a park, a place where they had shared countless memories and where their love had blossomed like the vibrant flowers that adorned the landscape. The park held a special significance for them, and he hoped it would serve as a place to reconnect.

As the day of the meeting arrived, he felt a mix of excitement and nervousness. The sun shone brightly, casting golden rays upon the green grass, as if nature itself was blessing their encounter. The gentle breeze rustled through the trees, creating a soothing rhythm that seemed to calm his anxious heart.

As he walked through the park, he looked around at the places he knew, hoping to catch a glimpse of her. As the leaves moved, the sun's light went through them and cast soft shadows on the path ahead. He finally saw her sitting on a worn-out bench near a peaceful pond, her eyes fixed on the mesmerising ripples on the surface of the water.

She had an ethereal beauty. She was wearing a flowy yellow sundress that matched the golden colours of the fall leaves. Her blonde hair was long and fell down her back. A simple ponytail kept it in place. He could tell that her emotions were heavy, and that her guardedness was a way to protect her hurt heart.

When they looked at each other across the park, the air was filled with a strong mix of nervousness and determination. His steps were shaky, and each one showed how important the conversation was going to be. She watched him closely with her arms crossed to protect herself. Her eyes showed that she was feeling a lot of different things.

He felt a lump in his throat as they got closer to each other. Memories—both good and bad—rushed through his mind, bringing him back to the past in a powerful way. Still, he knew he had to deal with the results of his actions and try to make up for the love he had lost.

"Hey, Sarah," he said, and his voice trembled with both fear and longing.

Sarah looked up; her face guarded but also a little bit curious. "Hi, Mark," she said, with a hint of caution in her voice.

They sat down on the worn-out wooden bench. The space between them was full of words they hadn't said and regrets that hadn't gone away. They were surrounded by a deep silence, as if time itself was holding its breath while waiting for the story of their shared past to come out.

He found the courage to speak, but his voice trembled under the weight of his mistakes. "Hey, I've been wanting to have a conversation with you," he said, his voice heavy with regret and sincerity. He paused to take a deep breath and gather his thoughts before continuing.

Her eyes met his, and in the whirlwind of mixed feelings, she looked into his eyes to see if he was being honest. She said, "Okay," with a tone that was cautious but open to the idea of understanding.

He felt better because she was willing to listen to him. He knew he had to show how sorry he was, not just say sorry. He wanted to say sorry in a way that went beyond words.

"I've spent a lot of nights thinking about myself," he said. His voice was steady but full of vulnerability. "I've come to realise how much my mistakes hurt others, and I'm fully committed to making things right."

His words hung in the air like thin threads of hope that were woven together. She listened carefully, her eyes getting softer and a little bit of curiosity showing through her tough exterior.

"I know that I caused you pain, Sarah. "And for that, I'm really sorry," he said. His voice was heavy with sincere regret. "My pride made it hard for me to see things clearly, so I pushed you away when I should have brought you closer. I was so focused on getting ahead that I forgot what really mattered."

Her face became even more relaxed, but there was still a hint of surprise in it. She uncrossed her arms, which was an unspoken sign that she was at least willing to try to understand.

"And how do you think we should fix what's broken?" Sarah asked, with a tone of cautious optimism in her voice. She looked into his eyes to see if he was being honest and if he really wanted to change

Mark looked at her straight in the eye as he pulled together his honesty. "I want to start small," he said in a serious tone of voice. "May I come over sometime for dinner? I want to spend time with our kids, to get to know them better and to show them that I will always be there for them.

His words hung in the air, full of hope and a desire to be forgiven. She thought about his request, her eyes moving back and forth between his face and the memories that still hurt her heart.

"You haven't cared about your kids in a long time. What has made you change your mind?" She asked, her voice a delicate mix of doubt and hope that showed how complicated her feelings were.

He took a moment to collect his thoughts. When he looked at her again, he did so with a mix of regret and determination in his eyes. " I've had some time to think about what I did and how much pain I caused. I realised how bad my mistakes were and how much damage I did to our relationship," he said, his voice full of sincerity. "I can't change what happened in the past, but I want to own up to what I did and try to make things right."

Her eyes softened as she listened to what he said, and her heart longed for healing and peace. "Mark, it's been a long and difficult journey for both of us," she said, her voice a mix of acceptance and cautious optimism. "Even though I can't take away the pain of the past, I'm willing to think about the possibility of moving on, not just for us but also for our children."

His eyes sparkled with hope as he listened to her answer. The weight of his guilt started to go away, and in its place was a hint of a new chance. "I can't tell you how thankful I am that you're willing to think about this," he said with sincere gratitude. "I know it won't be easy, but I'm committed to working hard, rebuilding trust, and being there for our children."

She nodded, and her face showed a mix of emotions. Even though they still had doubts, the idea that their kids might have a chance at a more peaceful family life was a powerful motivator. "Let's take it one step at a time," she said, with both caution and hope in her voice. "I'll need some time to think about everything, but I'll keep you updated and keep an open mind as we go through this together." He lowered his shoulders, and his face showed a mix of gratitude and anxiety. "Thank you. I really appreciate that you both gave me this chance. I also want to recognise and respect your new husband's role in the lives of our children," he said with a voice full of genuine gratitude.

Her smile became more real, and she looked up with a hint of hope in her eyes. She said, "He knows how important family is, and he wants our kids to have a good relationship with their dad." "Let's start with dinner and see where that takes us."

As they talked more, the atmosphere changed from tense to cautiously hopeful. People were talking and laughing in the park, and the sunlight was shining through the trees and warming their faces.

He said, "Thank you," and his thanks came through in his voice. "Your help means everything to me. I'll stop letting my pride get in the way. I'm going to be the kind of father our kids deserve."

Her voice got softer as she said, "I hope so." Her eyes showed a hint of forgiveness and a flash of the love they used to have for each other. In that park, where insects buzzed and leaves rustled, two souls found comfort in the idea that they could get better. The environment seemed to respond as well, with the insects making a soft melody and the leaves rustling as if they were excited.

He gave her his handkerchief, which she took with a soft smile. Tears and memories mixed together, and in that shared weakness, they found a weak bond. In the busy, peaceful park, they were no longer two hearts that had grown apart. Instead, they were two people who were tied together by the complexities of love and loss.

Together, they sat on the old bench with tears in their eyes as the park welcomed them on their way to healing and peace. As the sun went down, it turned the sky gold and pink, and they started the tricky process of putting back together what had been broken, with hearts that dared to hope for a second chance.

As the sun slowly set, casting a beautiful golden glow over the park, they were caught up in a whirlwind of feelings. The weight of their past together, including bittersweet memories and unspoken regrets, hung in the air between them like a fragile tapestry.

As a silent witness to their tumultuous reunion, the park seemed to hold its breath, as if it knew how important the moment was that was happening in its soft embrace. The rustling leaves told stories of forgiveness and second chances, while the buzzing of the insects matched the rhythm of their reconnected hearts.

She never took her eyes off of him. She was looking for signs of the man she used to love. The lines on his forehead and the tired look in his eyes told a lot about the journey he had been on, the lessons he had learned, and how humble he had become.

He spoke softly, and his voice was full of sincerity. His words carried the weight of his heart. "I want you to know that the mistakes I've made have kept me up many nights. The pain I caused you and our kids has made my heart heavy. I can't change what happened in the past, but I'll do whatever it takes to make things right."

His words, which were full of weakness, echoed through her body and woke up a lot of feelings that had been dormant for a long time. She felt her heart slowly start to open up, letting a glimmer of hope seep through the cracks in her tough exterior.

"I've never stopped loving you," he said with a hint of desperation in his voice. "But I know that love alone can't fix the damage I've done. I'm willing to do what it takes to win back your trust and show that I'm serious about being the partner and father our family needs."

Her eyes sparkled with tears as she listened. Her heart was torn between the pain of the past and a small spark of hope for a better future. She had made a new life for herself and found happiness in the arms of someone else, but her love for Mark still rang in her heart.

Her voice shook with distress and longing as she finally said, "I can't deny the love that once bound us." "But trust is hard to rebuild, and forgiving each other is a process that takes time and work from both of us."

He nodded, and his eyes showed that he was both determined and sorry. "I understand. I know it won't be easy to get back together with you. It will take time, understanding, and a willingness to face the truth about our past."

The park seemed to react to their touching conversation. The insects buzzed with a renewed sense of energy, creating a symphony of resilience and forgiveness. The leaves rustled as they embraced the winds of change. It was as if they were echoing the ideas of growth and change.

Her voice, which was soft but firm, rang out in the peaceful setting. "I believe in the power of second chances. But we have to be careful because our hearts are fragile and our decisions will affect our children.

He nodded, and his eyes were filled with thanks and a new sense of purpose. "Our children deserve to see us together, to see that love is strong enough to weather even the worst storms. I promise to be there for them, to make up for the time I didn't spend with them, and to give them a stable, caring place to live."

As their voices mixed with the sounds of nature, the park seemed to breathe out, letting go of the tension it had been holding. The gentle breeze carried their whispered promises and spread them out like seeds of hope, planting the possibility of a future built on love and understanding.

They sat in silence, feeling the weight of their promise to each other. Her tears were mixed with a smile, which showed how complicated their feelings were. Mark could tell that the mood was changing, so he reached out and gently took her hand. His touch brought her comfort and reassurance.

At that moment, surrounded by the quiet sounds of nature and the echoes of their past, they found comfort in the fact that their love, even though it was old and had scars, still had the power to fix what was broken. And as they sat together in the park, a feeling of new beginnings and second chances came over them, fighting to tie their lives together again.

THIRTEEN

A deep sense of relief and joy filled his heart when he heard the news from his sister. A glimmer of hope for reconciliation appeared to replace the weight that had weighed down their friendship. He had taken his advice and gotten in touch with his sister to apologise. This action gave Alex a renewed sense of happiness.

His faith in the efficacy of pardon and second chances was confirmed when he saw that Mark had made the first move towards mending the harm he had caused. Alex's confidence in their friendship was further reaffirmed by his attentive listening and subsequent actions.

He picked up his phone and immediately dialled his number. His tone was light as he spoke with him, and it was clear that he was genuinely happy. As a sign of their cherished friendship.

His voice was warm and grateful, saying, "I just heard from Rachel, and I want you to know how relieved and happy I am." "It means a lot that you reached to her and apologised as well. It demonstrates your dedication to making things right and your continued value in our friendship.

"Alex, there is nothing I desire more than to reconnect and rebuild what we once had," he said in a sincere and appreciative reply. I sincerely regret my errors and am appreciative of the chance to put things right.

As the discussion went on, his relief turned into intense joy. Knowing that he had taken the necessary actions to appease Rachel and mend their friendship's broken bonds, he felt a renewed sense of trust and confidence in him.

Alex smiled at the thought of sitting together, eating a meal, and having a meaningful conversation. He imagined the stories, the laughter, and the rekindling of shared memories that would happen all night long.

He could tell that he was being serious on the phone at that very moment. He was interested in what he had to say because his words had weight and sincerity. he said, "Hello, Mark," in a tone that was both sincere and excited. "I wanted to talk with you about something."

His heart skipped a beat as he replied, "Sure, what's on your mind?" He couldn't stop thinking about what could have caused him and his best friend to talk so seriously.

Alex's voice got softer, and it sounded like he understood and could forgive. "I want you to know that I forgive you, too," he said softly. "I know you've made mistakes, but I can see that you really want to get better. I'm glad you did that."

As he thought about what Alex had said, a wave of relief came over him. He was worried about losing his friendship, but now he saw a chance to make things better between them. "Thank you, Alex," he said, his voice full of thanks and a slight shake showing how he felt.

They kept talking, and time didn't seem to matter as they caught up on each other's lives and talked about old times. The faint sounds of children playing could be heard in the background through the phone line. This reminded Alex of the full life he had built for himself.

His voice filled with excitement all of a sudden. "I have a thought!" he yelled. "Why don't you come to dinner with us this evening? It would be great to meet you in person, and with my wife we can all sit down and catch up."

He felt a rush of happiness when he said yes to the invite. It was a chance to not only enjoy a tasty meal, but also talk to each other again after they had grown apart. He realised how much he had missed Alex's warm presence and the strong bond they used to have.

Mark smiled and eagerly agreed, ready to take advantage of this chance to make things right and rebuild a friendship that meant a lot to him. He said, a genuine smile spreading across his face, "Sure, I'd love to come over."

He felt hopeful again when he thought about an evening full of good food, laughter, and deep conversations. As soon as he hung up the phone, he felt more hopeful about their future.

Gratitude overcame him as he ended the call. He was appreciative of Mark's willingness to listen, think, and act. This act of forgiveness not only restored his relationship with his sister but also reaffirmed his faith in the strength of their friendship and the efficacy of personal development and forgiveness.

He looked forward to the upcoming dinner with a lighter heart, once more treating Mark as an old friend. He was aware that their process of re-establishing trust and strengthening their relationship would continue to develop little by little.

As he concluded his phone call with Alex, a profound sense of gratitude filled his heart. Though he recognized the journey ahead was still long, he couldn't help but feel a surge of optimism, finally witnessing the progress he had been longing for.

While the sun gracefully descended beneath the horizon, casting a warm, golden glow upon his residence in Toronto, he reached for his phone and dialed a number. It had been months since they last conversed, and his heart fluttered with anticipation as he eagerly awaited the familiar voice of his friend on the other end of the line.

His hand felt the familiar vibration of his phone thousands of miles away in Lagos, Nigeria. It was the end of a busy day, and the energy of the city was still in the air. The busy streets, loud conversations, and honking cars made a rhythmic symphony that went well with the soothing sounds of crickets and the warm breeze caressing the palm trees outside his window.

As he picked up the call, a mixture of excitement and nostalgia saturated the airwaves. "Mark! It's a pleasure to hear your voice," he exclaimed, his words resonating with the distinct cadence of his Nigerian heritage.

His smile broadened as he replied, "Arinze, my dear friend! It has been far too long. How have you been since your return to Nigeria?"

He paused for a moment; his mind flooded with memories of adjusting to life in Lagos. "It has been quite the adventure, my friend," he replied, his voice a medley of fondness and resilience. "Nigeria has embraced us with open arms, and we have been navigating the joys and challenges that come with living in this vibrant city."

As their conversation unfolded, the unique soundscape of each location painted a vivid backdrop. In Toronto, the gentle hum of city life intertwined with occasional distant sirens, while the crispness in the air heralded the arrival of autumn, with leaves rustling underfoot, adorning the landscape with vibrant shades of red and gold.

Meanwhile, in Lagos, a symphony of street vendors, car horns, and laughter provided a pulsating backdrop. The rhythm of life in the city resonated through his words, as he eloquently described the energy and liveliness that defined Lagos. The warm evening breeze carried with it the tantalizing scent of street food, accompanied by the rhythmic chirping of crickets.

They both delved into a rich cross-stitch of conversation, catching up on the intricacies of their lives. They shared stories of family, work, and the challenges they had encountered since their last meeting. Each word carried the weight of their shared history, a testament to the enduring bond they had nurtured over the years.

As the conversation progressed, both couldn't help but reflect on the stark differences between their current environments. His thoughts drifted to the tranquility and orderliness of Toronto, where the changing seasons brought a sense of familiarity and structure. He couldn't help but yearn for the serene tranquility of his Canadian home.

Meanwhile, his mind wandered to the pulsating energy of Lagos—the vibrant markets, the lively street scenes, and the warmth of the Nigerian people. He marveled at the resilience and resourcefulness of his fellow citizens, finding solace and purpose in the unique challenges that Nigeria presented.

Amidst their reflections, a shared sense of admiration and curiosity emerged. Mark yearned to experience the vibrant chaos of Lagos, immersing himself in the rich cultural drapery that Arinze so vividly described. Likewise, Arinze felt a yearning for the tranquility and orderliness of

Toronto, envisioning the serenity that accompanied the changing seasons.

And so, during the course of their conversation, he extended an invitation. "My friend, why don't you come to Nigeria? Experience the beauty of Lagos firsthand. It would be wonderful to have you here."

His heart beat faster when he thought about it. He couldn't pass up the chance to see a new world and reconnect with his best friend in Nigeria, where they had just moved. He accepted Arinze's invitation with a mix of excitement and determination. Their shared excitement helped bridge the gap between their worlds.

As the call drew to a close, they promised to reconnect soon, energized by the prospect of their upcoming reunion in Lagos. The familiar sound of their laughter filled the air, transcending time and space.

With a renewed sense of connection, they bid each other farewell, knowing that their journey would not only deepen their friendship but also expand their understanding of the world they now resided in.

FOURTEEN

After concluding the call, he glanced at his wristwatch, his eyes widening in realization. He had completely forgotten about the dinner invitation from his friend Alex. With a mix of excitement and haste, he rushed to prepare for the evening. Opting for a sleek, charcoal gray suit, he carefully paired it with a crisp white shirt and a stylish tie.

Feeling a sense of urgency, he hastily combed his hair and checked his appearance in the mirror before heading out the door.

As he stood on the doorstep of Alex's beautiful home, he was filled with awe. The two-story house was really grand, with a big front yard and well-kept gardens. The entrance's intricately carved wooden doors gave off an air of elegance and sophistication, showing that he had good taste.

He took a deep breath to calm his excitement and rang the doorbell. With each passing second, his excitement grew. When the door opened, a person in a sleek black suit was there. It was Chen, Alex's trusted servant who had been a part of the family for a long time and was always there.

"Good evening, sir. Welcome to the Sinclair residence," John greeted with a polite nod and an outstretched hand, leading him inside with graceful movements.

Warm light from the windows danced on the polished brass doorknob, sending sparkling reflections all around the luxurious room. He couldn't help but be amazed by how Alex's taste and attention to detail were reflected in every part of the house.

"You truly are a master at your craft, Chen," he remarked, impressed by how well the servant did his job.

"Thank you, sir. It's an honor to serve the Sinclair family," he replied humbly.

As they went deeper into the beautiful mansion, his excitement grew, and he was filled with a wonderful mix of curiosity and wonder. The evening's events were about to start, which promised to be a magical time inside this stately home.

Every move the servant made showed how dedicated he was to his job and how well he paid attention to details. Each move had a sense of grace and precision, which showed how hardworking and skilled the people in his household were. He couldn't help but be impressed by how well he did his job, and he liked the ease with which he handled his tasks.

Crossing the threshold into the grand house, he felt warm and excited as he stepped inside. As he went deeper into the luxurious home, Alex and Emily's lively voices filled the air. Their faces were lit up with joy and excitement. Her eyes lit up with happiness as she ran towards him and gave him a tight hug that showed how close they were. The warmth of her welcome was shared by everyone in the house, bringing Mark into a small group of close friends.

"Mark! Finally, you're here! We've missed you so much!" Emily exclaimed.

"I've missed you both too! This place is incredible!" he replied, beaming with joy.

He felt more than just a passing familiarity with the people around him as they laughed and talked loudly.

Alex's loud laughter echoed through the large rooms, and every so often, he gave him a firm pat on the back, as if to confirm the deep friendship that had grown between them. It felt like they had never been apart, and their embrace made time and distance disappear.

"Mark, my man! It's been too long! How have you been?" Alex asked.

"I've been good, Alex! Can't believe how much time has passed since we last hung out," he replied.

At that moment, when the air was full of laughter and love, he knew that he had not just walked into a house, but also a safe place full of warmth, friendship, and memories. The magical night held the promise of deeper connections and long-lasting bonds. It reminded him of how much true friendship is worth.

The room was filled with genuine warmth and happiness, which set the stage for an unforgettable evening. It was as if the whole universe had come together to make the perfect atmosphere for celebration and coming together. He felt right at home as soon as his good friends wrapped their arms around him. It was as if he had come back to a place he had never really left.

As the guests walked to the elegant dining room, each step seemed to be filled with excitement and anticipation. The room itself was a show of good taste and easy elegance. It was filled with delicate decorations and lit by the soft glow of flickering candles. Laughter, conversation, and the sound of glasses clinking together created a symphony of happiness that filled the air.

Everyone found a place at the table, which was set up beautifully. The dancing flames lit up their faces. He looked around the room, amazed by how beautiful and bright his hosts and other guests were. Conversations flowed like a gentle river, making a tapestry of shared experiences out of stories and laughter. A genuine sense of friendship and connection was created by the mix of playful banter and sincere admiration.

The couple, who were the best kind of hosts, couldn't hold back their excitement as they told stories about their own adventures and successes. Their voices carried the melody of happy memories, and their eyes shone with a joy that was contagious. He couldn't help but be drawn in by their genuine happiness, and his words showed how proud he was of what they had done.

Emily leaned closer to him in a quiet moment of closeness. Her voice was a soft whisper among the other voices. She told him, "Dear, you have no idea how much we've missed you." Her words were full of warmth and sincerity. "It means so much to us that you're here with us tonight."

His heart was full of gratitude, and he felt a deep sense of connection with the other people there. Laughter and companionship filled the air. As the night went on, he realised that this reunion was more than just a group of friends getting together. It was a sign of how strong friendships can be and how much joy can be found in the company of people who care.

Touched by her words, he smiled warmly. "Thank you, Emily. I've missed you both as well. This evening feels like a reunion filled with laughter and love."

The room became lively with warm hugs, sincere compliments, and joyful laughter. Their friendship brought harmony, and they formed genuine connections in this cheerful atmosphere.

As the evening progressed, him and his hosts reveled in the enchantment of the gathering, cherishing each moment shared. It was an evening where time seemed to stand still, and the bonds of friendship were reaffirmed.

❖

The dinner was like a beautifully choreographed ballet, where the delicate dance of flavours and the symphony of conversations went hand in hand. Each course, which was carefully planned and presented with care, led to interesting conversations and new ideas. They found themselves in the middle of an evening that perfectly combined their shared love of great food and thought-provoking conversations.

As they were getting ready to sit down at the table, a colourful salad of mixed greens greeted them. The plate, which was like an artist's canvas, had a mix of colours that caught their attention right away. Fresh lettuce leaves with their emerald colours danced around bright red tomatoes, and the toasted almonds added a delightful crunch. It was a beautiful work of art that made everyone in the room whisper praise and awe.

"Oh, I must say I'm incredibly impressed by the care and creativity you put into each part of this dish," he exclaimed, genuine admiration in his voice.

Emily smiled, pleased by the compliment, "Thank you. We love experimenting with flavors and presenting dishes in an artistic way."

"It really shows," He replied, taking another bite. "The way the ingredients come together is a true testament to your culinary skills and dedication."

Alex beamed, "We're glad you're enjoying it! The vinaigrette and toasted almonds are some of our favorite touches."

"They're fantastic!" Mark agreed, his taste buds rejoicing in the symphony of flavors.

As they continued eating, the conversation flowed naturally, accompanied by the clinking of cutlery and the hum of contentment. He found himself captivated by the depth and breadth of knowledge shared around the table.

"You two not only have a talent for cooking but also for sparking engaging discussions," He noted, impressed by the diverse topics they covered.

Emily chuckled, "We enjoy sharing ideas and experiences with our guests. It makes the meal even more memorable."

"Absolutely," he said, his curiosity piqued. "From culinary adventures to profound musings, this evening has been enriching."

Alex nodded, "That's what we love about gatherings like this. It's not just about the food; it's about the connections we make and the stories we share."

He felt a genuine connection with his hosts, knowing that their shared passion for good food and stimulating conversations had brought them closer together.

"This has been a truly wonderful experience," he said sincerely. "I feel so grateful to have been invited to this gathering."

She smiled warmly, "We're grateful to have you here, Mark. It's been a pleasure to have you here and sharing this evening with you over dinner."

He raised his glass, "Here's to the power of great food and meaningful conversations!"

"To the power of great food and meaningful conversations!" Alex and Emily echoed, clinking their glasses with Mark's.

With a sly grin, Alex leaned in closer and said, "Be careful with those almonds," in Mark's ear. They frequently disappear under mysterious circumstances, especially when she is nearby.

She chuckled before giving him a playful prod. Oh, please, I beg you! I just can't resist the crunch. She added some humour to the situation by remarking, "It's almost as if they have a mystical allure.

The sound of their contagious laughter filled the room with their merriment and goodwill. He enjoyed the verdant crispness of the greens and the flavorful harmony of the dish as a whole as he savoured each bite.

The aroma of roasted chicken, which was served with a variety of fresh seasonal vegetables and velvety mashed potatoes, filled the space when it was time for the main course. The chicken was perfectly cooked, giving it a tender and succulent texture.

"I have to admit, Alex's special marinade is what elevates this chicken to a whole new level, she leaned in close and whispered conspiratorially in his ear. Where else will you be able to find a roast of this calibre?

He replied, "Well, Emily, I might have to kidnap Alex and bring him to my kitchen," with a sly grin on his face. I must be informed of that top-secret recipe!

They had fun bantering with one another, which made the meal even more enjoyable. The flavours dancing on his tongue couldn't help but make him feel appreciative. These flavours served as a testament to their skill and attention to detail in the kitchen.

The dessert was a rich chocolate mousse with a drizzle of caramel and a variety of fresh berries on top. The way the presentation was done was very classy. Each bite was a luscious symphony of decadence, with the velvety texture of the mousse blending perfectly with the sweetness of the caramel and the burst of freshness from the berries. With each bite, it was like hearing a beautiful symphony.

As the sweet flavours of the dessert danced on their tongues, the talk at the table became more serious. Each person had their own political views, and these began to shape the conversation about Canadian politics.

Mark, who really cared about the Green Party, leaned forward and spoke with a lot of passion. "Climate change is the defining issue of our time," he said. "We need to be brave if we want to protect our planet and make sure that future generations will have a good life. I agree with the Green Party's focus on clean energy and conservation, and I think we need even more ambitious policies to fight climate change.

Emily, a strong supporter of the Liberal Party, nodded in agreement. She said, "I appreciate what the government is doing to support environmental initiatives." "Justin Trudeau's support for the Paris Agreement and investments in clean energy are good steps. But we also need to make sure that decision-making is open and includes everyone if we want to really address the concerns of all Canadians.

Alex, a loyal Conservative Party supporter, raised an eyebrow as he paid close attention. "I share your concerns about the environment," he said, "but we need to find a balance between protecting the environment and making the economy grow." We need policies that help create jobs and promote long-term growth. It's about finding solutions that help both our economy and the environment."

The conversation went back and forth as each person shared their ideas and debated them in a polite way. They talked about how complicated climate change is and how the government is doing and what it is doing about it. Their voices were full of passion, conviction, and a real desire to make a difference for the better.

They shared quotes and counterarguments, and the table was full of intellectual energy. Even though they had different political views, they had a sense of friendship and a common goal. They knew that their main goal was to see Canada have a better future.

At that moment, their different points of view came together in a way that worked well, making a rich needlepoint of ideas and possibilities. They talked late into the night about other important problems facing the country. Their voices echoed with the hope of finding common ground and making a way to a better tomorrow.

During the intellectual conversation, He took a deep breath and opened up about his own life. "You know, guys," he began, looking at Emily and Alex, "I've been doing a lot of self-reflection lately, and I can't help but regret some things about the end of my marriage."

They both listened attentively, their eyes showing genuine care and support.

"It takes courage to talk about these things," she said, her voice encouraging.

He nodded, feeling a sense of relief in being able to share his feelings. "Yeah, it's not easy admitting your mistakes and shortcomings, but I want to be open and humble about it. I want to grow as a person and make amends."

"That's commendable," Alex chimed in. "We all have our struggles, and being able to acknowledge them is the first step towards positive change."

As the conversation continued, they delved even deeper into their own lives, sharing their vulnerabilities and experiences. The atmosphere was one of understanding and acceptance, and they listened to each other with care and empathy.

"It's incredible how powerful these conversations can be," Mark mused. "We're using each other's knowledge and experiences to learn and grow."

"You're right," she agreed. "It's essential to reflect on our lives and be humble enough to learn from one another."

"I feel like our friendship is getting stronger because we're all committed to personal growth and facing life's challenges together," Mark said, a sense of gratitude in his voice.

At Alex's house, they shared not just serious discussions but also light-hearted jokes, creating a genuine sense of community. The warmth of their interactions seemed to seep into the walls, fostering an environment that encouraged more sincere connections and conversations.

"I'm so grateful for both of you," he said, smiling at his friends. "This evening has been so enriching, both intellectually and emotionally."

"We're grateful for you too," Alex replied warmly. "It's amazing how much we can learn and support each other when we're open and honest."

His joy and excitement were obvious on his face as he told them his news. Hey, guys, what do you know? I received an invitation from Arinze to visit Nigeria. After giving it some thought, I've made the decision to use my upcoming weeks of vacation time to travel.

Her eyes widened and her brows furrowed, giving off a more worried appearance. "Nigeria? Africa? Mark, that was a pretty big leap. According to the stories I've heard, there appear to be many unpredictable issues and safety concerns there. I'm worried."

He was unyielding about assuaging her worries despite the fact that he could understand them. "I understand your concern, Emily, but you must trust what I am saying. At this point, my friend and his family have lived in Nigeria for a while. He is very knowledgeable about the area, and I know I can trust him to lead me safely and in the right direction.

Alex, who is renowned for being the voice of reason, supported the contention. "I recognise Emily's concerns, but don't overlook the amazing adventures and cultural enrichment Nigeria has in store for you. It will blow your mind; I can assure you of that. Through this experience, you have the chance to broaden your horizons and develop your friendship with Arinze. Just make sure you keep yourself informed and heed his advice while you're there.

He agreed by nodding his head, his confidence unflappable. "Alex, you're 100 percent right. I've done my research, and Arinze has promised to treat me just like one of his own family members. I've made the decision to travel because I trust my instincts and want to fully experience Nigeria's beauty and originality. It provides an opportunity for both my personal growth and for me to reconnect with a friend.

She couldn't help herself, she had to express her lingering worries. "Make a solemn promise to me, Mark, that you will keep watch and take the necessary precautions. My main priority is making sure you're okay.

He held out his hand to Emily, reassuring her by holding her hand tenderly as his eyes welled up with understanding. you have my word. I will proceed cautiously at every turn and completely rely on Arinze's guidance. Together, we'll learn about the local way of life and make sure my trip is both fun and educational. You need not worry about anything at all.

The three of them continued their conversation as they attempted to strike a balance between his resolve and her concerns. Every word they spoke was an expression of their genuine love and unwavering support for one another. The bonds of friendship between them tightened right then and there as they sat around the table, and their mutual trust served as an anchor for them in the face of uncertainty.

FIFTEEN

His trip from Toronto to Ottawa was fraught with worry and unease on account of the fact that he was getting ready to submit his visa application to the Nigerian Embassy in Ottawa. His worries were compounded by the fact that he had previously heard accounts that detailed the bureaucracy and corruption that existed in Nigeria. Even though the drive itself was beautiful, His thoughts kept going back to the stories he'd heard about Nigeria and Africa in general while he was on the road.

As he entered the imposing structure of the Nigerian Embassy in Ottawa, he couldn't help but notice the numerous precautions taken for his safety. The tall walls, cameras, and watchful security personnel reflected the stringent scrutiny that is associated with visa applications for the Nigerian government. The queue of people waiting to enter the embassy was long and crowded with people who were visibly nervous. The environment was tense, and there was a palpable air of impatience and frustration in the conversations that took place around him.

He struck up a conversation with a woman standing next to him in the queue. "Hi, my name is Mark. Are you also applying for a visa to Nigeria?" he asked.

"Yes, I am. My name is Aisha. I'm a Nigerian citizen who has been living in Canada for several years. I'm going to visit my family in Nigeria," Aisha replied.

"That's great. I've heard that the visa application process can be quite challenging. Have you applied for a visa before?" he asked.

"Yes, I have. The process can be time-consuming and difficult, but I'm hoping it won't be too bad this time," Aisha said.

As he made his way to the office where he could submit his application for a visa, he encountered a man who was also applying for a visa. "Excuse me, do you know how long the wait is?" the man asked.

"I'm not sure, but I've heard that it can take several hours. Are you also applying for a visa to Nigeria?" Mark asked.

"Yes, I am. My name is Ahmed. I'm going to Nigeria for a business trip," Ahmed replied.

"I see. I'm Mark. I'm applying for a visa to visit a friend in Nigeria," he said.

As he stood in line at the Nigerian embassy, he couldn't help but feel overwhelmed by the time-consuming and challenging visa application process. "I've prepared everything carefully," he whispered to himself, glancing at the stack of forms and documents in his hands.

Just ahead of him, a fellow applicant turned to Mark with a sympathetic smile. "It's a bit of a maze, isn't it?" she said, her voice tinged with frustration.

Mark nodded, grateful for the camaraderie. "Definitely. I thought I had everything, but they keep asking for more and more."

As they continued chatting, he couldn't help but notice the cultural differences that made this embassy experience unique. "It's so different from what I'm used to in other countries embassy," he mused.

"I know what you mean," the woman replied. "Patience and understanding go a long way here. It's a whole different ballgame."

As he navigated the complex bureaucracy, he couldn't shake off the feeling of being out of his comfort zone. "I never thought dealing with paperwork could be this challenging," he admitted.

"Just take a deep breath," the woman advised, offering a reassuring pat on the back. "You'll get through it. We all do."

The hours passed, and his anxiety grew as he awaited his turn to submit his application. "I've heard stories about bribery and corruption," he confided to the woman. "I hope my application will be treated fairly."

"I understand your concern," she said, her eyes reflecting empathy. "We all hope for the best."

After the embassy finally approved his application, he was able to leave and start his journey back to Toronto. Throughout the trip, he couldn't help but ponder the striking contrast between his experiences at the Nigerian embassy and those he had encountered in other countries while obtaining visas.

Later that day, he met up with his friend Esther and recounted his experience. "It was quite a challenge," he told her, shaking his head.

Esther listened attentively. "It must have been tough dealing with the bureaucracy and cultural differences," she said, trying to grasp the gravity of the situation.

"It really was," he agreed. "I wish it could be smoother for everyone applying for visas."

"I hope things improve in the future," Esther said, her voice filled with hope. "It's essential for a country to have efficient processes and combat corruption."

He nodded, feeling grateful for Esther's understanding. "Absolutely. These difficulties are a symptom of deeper issues that need to be addressed."

As he drove back on the highway, he had plenty of time to reflect, contemplating the need for change and progress in Nigeria. Despite the frustrations he experienced at the Nigerian embassy, he couldn't help but be impressed with how fast his visa was approved in contrast to other countries' embassies he had been to. He longed for a time when those applying for visas in Nigerian embassies would have a simpler and more streamlined experience, akin to the efficient process he had observed at other countries' embassies.

It's frustrating to see how much corruption and bureaucracy can hold back a country," he said to himself. While acknowledging that the visa process in Nigeria was better than some other countries he had experienced, he couldn't shake off the disappointment with the embassy's system. It still seemed to be burdened with superfluous obstacles and corrupt practices that hampered the process.

As he continued his journey back to Toronto, his thoughts shifted to a vision of a more efficient and transparent embassy system for Nigeria. He strongly believed that there was room for improvement. They could eliminate unnecessary queues and implement online passport renewal and visa issuance processes to expedite the entire procedure.

His words reflected not only frustration but also a sincere hope for a brighter future for Nigeria. He yearned for the nation to make significant progress, offering its citizens a smoother and more streamlined embassy experience. He believed that such positive changes in the government and society would contribute to the overall growth and prosperity of the nation.

SIXTEEN

They found a quiet spot in the middle of a busy office cafeteria to talk about his trip to Nigeria during their lunch break. His coworker Chiamaka was full of energy as he told her about his plans for the future and asked for her feedback and ideas.

She took an energetic stance, and her eyes were wide with excitement. "Mark, your trip to Nigeria is going to be fantastic! There are a lot of interesting things to do in the country. You should visit exciting cities like Lagos and Calabar, where the excitement spreads."

He gave her words his full attention and nodded. He said, "I can't wait to learn everything I can about Nigeria's rich culture. And what's the food like? I've heard amazing things about the food in Nigeria."

Her smile was a little bit sneaky. "Oh, what a treat it is to eat Nigerian food! You have to try some of the local food, like pounded yam served with egusi soup, suya, and the world-famous jollof rice.

He laughed and nodded to show that he was aware of the ongoing debate about jollof rice. "Ah, yes! I know a lot about that subject. It is a very controversial topic. But you know, thanks to Arinze I've had the chance to taste jollof rice from both Nigeria and Ghana."

She was getting more and more interested as time went on. "Really? You've tried both of them, right? How are they different?"

He put his shoulders back and thought about all the different foods he had tried. "Well, I have to say that both versions, which were delicious in their own ways, were very good. The Nigerian jollof rice had a rich, slightly smokey flavour, and it was cooked perfectly so that each grain kept its own shape. Every bite was an explosion of different tastes. On the other hand, the jollof rice served in Ghana has a unique mix of spices that makes it taste different and aromatic.

She nodded and listened carefully as he told the story. "It sounds like a really fun thing to do. I'm glad you had the chance to try both and see how different they are."

He smiled at her and agreed with her completely. "Absolutely! We shouldn't ask which jollof rice is better; instead, we should celebrate the different ways that both countries cook and their rich culinary histories. The fact that each one has its own taste and cultural meaning makes the discussion even more fun."

She nodded to show that he agreed. " You're right on the money. The jollof rice debate is a fun way to show how much we all love this beloved dish. It also shows how food can bring people together.

His excitement grew as he thought about the food adventure that was waiting for him. "I will do that for sure! Do you have any more suggestions or advice?"

As she moved closer, her voice got more animated, signifying her intent to communicate effectively. "Of course, Mark. Accept and take part in the region's cultural practises. Nigerians are known for being friendly and helpful, so don't be afraid to talk to people there. You can also learn about the country's rich history by going to places like Benin City and getting lost in its beautiful natural scenery. If you can, you should try to go to a traditional festival, which is a lively celebration of our heritage."

He nodded and thought about what she had said. "Thank you. Your ideas have been extremely helpful. I can't wait to see Nigeria through Arinze's eyes and learn about all the wonderful things your country has to offer."

She was happy and proud, and her eyes were bright. "Thank you for understanding. I'm sure that your time in Nigeria will be something you'll never forget. Enjoy the thrills, savour the delicious moments, and make memories that will last a lifetime. And always remember that Nigeria has its own special magic when it comes to jollof rice!"

As they talked, the room was filled with their excitement. Together, they excitedly planned and talked about his upcoming trip, getting caught up in the joy of learning about Nigeria's vibrant culture and rich history. He was getting more and more excited about his trip to Nigeria.

I can't wait to go to Nigeria and eat the real jollof rice." But I've been hearing about security problems, especially kidnappings, in different parts of the country, which has made me a little worried.

She nodded understandingly to show that she understood Mark's worries. "Yes, Mark, sometimes I worry about your safety in Nigeria. It is important to be careful and get as much information as you can. But also remember that stories about these kinds of things are often exaggerated. The news tends to focus on bad things, which makes it hard to see the many safe and friendly places in the country.

He listened to what she said and felt a little less worried. "I see. So, what should I do to keep myself safe while I'm there?"

Her voice became more reassuring. "First and foremost, it's important that you take your host advice. He knows the area's terrain well and can lead you to safe places. Don't stay alone, especially in places you don't know. Stay up-to-date on travel advisories and talk to locals to find out the most recent information about certain areas."

She continued, "It's also very important that you stay alert, lock up your things, and don't put valuable things out in the open." Choose reliable ways to get around, and stay in well-known, safe neighbourhoods.

He listened carefully and agreed that her advice was good. He learned how important it was to find a balance between being careful and being open-minded, so that he could experience Nigeria without being frozen by fear.

He thanked her saying, "Thank you." Your point of view and helpful safety tips have helped me understand the situation better. I will definitely follow Arinze's advice and take the necessary precautions to make sure my trip is fun and goes smoothly.

She smiled back in a friendly way. "Thank you for understanding. If you have the right attitude and take the safety precautions you need, you will have a great time in Nigeria. There is a lot to do and see in the country. Accept the friendliness of the people there, learn as much as you can about the culture, and make the most of your trip. Arinze will be there to show off everything Nigeria has to offer.

He got more excited as they talked and was determined to start his trip with a balanced mind, ready to make memories in Nigeria while keeping in mind the safety concerns that come with going anywhere.

SEVENTEEN

He really wanted to go to Nigeria, so he planned his flight from Toronto to Lagos very carefully. He chose to go on his trip with the well-known airline Air Dove. As the day of departure got closer, he was getting more and more excited.

He went to Toronto Pearson International Airport on the day he was supposed to leave. This airport is a busy place for international flights. People were busy at the airport, which was well known for its modern facilities and smooth operations. As he walked into the departure area, he was amazed by how well-planned and organised everything was.

He was patient while his passport and other travel documents were checked at the immigration checkpoints. Immigration officers carefully checked each passenger and made sure that everyone was safe. He went to the security checks when he was given the all-clear. He put his things in trays and went through the scanners. On the other side, he got his things. As he got ready to board his flight, he felt safe because he knew there would be strict security.

He had to finally get on the Air Dove flight to Lagos. As soon as he sat down, he noticed how cosy the cabin was and how friendly the flight attendants were. He told the flight attendant, "I'm so happy to be going to Nigeria. So much has been said about the country, and I can't wait to see it for myself." "We're glad to have you on board, sir," the flight attendant said with a smile. We hope you have a pleasant flight."

The airline went out of its way to make sure passengers had a good time. This was clear from the friendly service and well-kept planes.

As he took his seat, he watched the flight attendants. With their friendly smiles and well-mannered ways, they made everyone feel at ease right away. The way they looked showed that they were confident and friendly. They helped the passengers by moving with grace and paying attention.

As people took their seats, the air was filled with excitement as they looked forward to the trip ahead. Most passengers seemed eager and curious. While some of them fastened their seat belts, others gazed out the window to observe the bustling airport tarmac.

The cabin lights got brighter; the crackling sound of the speakers caught everyone's attention. As heads turned towards the sound, the cabin went from being busy to being focused and ready. When the captain's voice came over the speaker, it made everyone feel calm.

"This is your captain speaking, ladies and gentlemen. We're glad to have you on Air Dove flight 753, which is going to Lagos, Nigeria. I'd like to tell you some important things about our trip. Please listen to me as we get ready to take off.

During our planned flight, we will stop for a short time in Addis Ababa. This stop is part of our plan, and it gives some passengers a chance to do something. Pay close attention, people who are going to Lagos, Nigeria.

Those of you who are going to Lagos will be able to switch to a separate Air Dove flight as soon as we get to Addis Ababa. Our helpful ground staff will be there to help you and make sure everything goes smoothly

When we land, our friendly flight attendants and ground staff will be there to help you find the right gate for your next flight or help you switch to a different plane if you need to. Rest assured that they will do their best to make your move as quick and easy as possible.

We know how important your comfort and ease of life are to you. I'd like to thank you on behalf of the whole crew for being patient and working with us during the connection and layover. We work hard to make sure that your trip goes smoothly.

We're glad you chose to fly with Air Dove. We're glad to have you join us. Enjoy the flight to your final destination, Lagos, Nigeria, and sit back, relax, and enjoy the journey."

The captain's voice stopped, making the passengers feel safe and excited for the trip that lay ahead.

Just before the plane took off, the diligent flight attendants, adorned in their impeccable uniforms and wearing warm smiles, strategically positioned themselves throughout the cabin. They made sure that each passenger had a clear view as they conducted a thorough demonstration of the air safety tips. The atmosphere inside the plane was charged with excitement, and the passengers attentively observed the informative presentation, ensuring everyone was well-prepared for a safe and enjoyable flight.

With a warm smile, one of the flight attendants positioned near the cockpit spoke into the intercom, ensuring her voice resonated throughout the entire cabin. "Good afternoon, everyone, and welcome to Air Dove flight 753. We're delighted to have you here with us today. Kindly fasten your seat belts, stow your tray tables, and ensure your seatbacks are in the upright position. Thank you for choosing Air Dove, and we wish you a safe and pleasant journey."

As the passengers settled into their seats, he couldn't help but notice the friendly man seated next to him. With a warm smile, the man greeted him, "Hello there, I'm Emeka. It's a pleasure to meet you."

He returned the greeting, "Nice to meet you too, Emeka. I'm Mark. Are you heading back home to Nigeria?"

His eyes sparkled with excitement, "Yes, I am! I've been away for quite some time, and I can't wait to be back with my family and friends. It's been too long."

He nodded in understanding, "I know what you mean. There's something special about going back home after being away for a while. It feels like a reunion filled with joy and longing."

Emeka agreed wholeheartedly, "Exactly! There's nothing quite like the feeling of being back in familiar surroundings and reconnecting with loved ones."

As the flight attendants went through the safety instructions, the two men listened attentively, exchanging brief glances and nodding in acknowledgment.

After the instructions, He turned to him with a curious expression. "Mark, if you don't mind me asking, you mentioned you usually fly in first class. What made you choose economy class this time?"

He chuckled, "Well, I wanted to experience something different this time. Flying in first class is comfortable and all, but I thought flying in economy would give me a chance to connect with fellow travelers and hear their stories."

He laughed heartily, "I see. That's a unique perspective. I've flown in economy many times, and it's always interesting to meet new people and share experiences."

He nodded, "Exactly! It's all about the journey and the connections we make along the way."

He leaned in, intrigued by Mark's choice. "So, how's your experience so far? Are you enjoying the different atmosphere in economy?"

He smiled, "I have to say, I'm loving it. There's a sense of friendship here, and I get to hear stories from travelers like you. It's been refreshing and eye-opening."

He grinned, "That's wonderful to hear! I'm glad you decided to try something new and have this conversation with me."

They kept talking as the plane picked up speed. They told each other stories and talked about how excited they were to go to Nigeria soon. Their conversation flowed easily as they told stories from their own lives and talked about the rich cultures and varied landscapes of their home countries.

The plane took off with a loud roar and went up into the sky. As the plane flew over Toronto's sprawling cityscape, Mark felt a gentle lift. The cityscape was soon replaced by a beautiful blue sky with fluffy clouds.

They continued their conversation as the flight progressed. Emeka talked about the delicious foods he couldn't wait to try again and how happy he was to see his family again. "I can't wait to have some pounded yam with egusi soup," he said with a smile.

He laughed. "I've heard so much about Nigerian food. I can't wait to try it for myself. And I'm really looking forward to seeing my friend Arinze again. It's been too long.

"Their conversation was interrupted by turbulence, which briefly jolted the plane and made the passengers tense for a short time. But the skilled pilots got the plane through the rough spots, and the calm attitude of the flight attendants made everyone feel better.

As the flight attendants moved gracefully up and down the aisles, meeting the needs of the passengers and bringing them drinks, they talked about their plans for their trip. "Arinze has a lot of things planned for us," Mark said. "We're going to visit Lagos, Abuja, and some of the other states.

"Emeka nodded. "Those are all great places to visit. Just be careful, though. Nigeria can be a bit unpredictable at times.

"He looked concerned. "What do you mean?

"He explained, "There are some safety concerns, especially in the northern and Middle Belt states. And there's always the risk of petty crime, like pickpocketing and theft. But as long as you're careful and take precautions, you should be okay.

"He nodded. "Thanks for the heads up. I'll make sure to be careful.

"As the journey continued, their conversation varied from light-hearted banter to serious discussions about the challenges facing Nigeria. They talked about the country's economy, its infrastructure, and its education system. They shared their thoughts on how to improve the situation and make Nigeria a better place for everyone.

As they made a brief stop in Addis Ababa, Mark was awestruck by the exquisite Ethiopian artwork and the pulsating traditional music. "This is amazing," he said to Emeka. "I've never seen anything like it.

"He grinned. "Ethiopia is a beautiful country with a rich cultural heritage. I'm glad you're enjoying it

Their conversation continued throughout the flight, with each person sharing their own unique perspective on life and the world around them.

As He started the last part of his journey with a rush of excitement that could be felt in his veins. With each passing minute, the excitement grew by a factor of a million. He couldn't help but notice the subtle change in the air, which meant the plane was about to land in Lagos, as the Air Dove flight got closer and closer to its destination.

The pilot's authoritative voice echoed through the cabin, breaking the quiet with an announcement. "Ladies and gentlemen, the beautiful city of Lagos, Nigeria, is coming up quickly. We'd like to politely ask you to fasten your seatbelts and put away your tray tables as we prepare to land. We really hope that your trip with Air Dove was a good one, and we thank you for choosing us as your favourite airline."

His eyes got very big when he looked out the window. Lagos, a huge city, spread out below him in a stunning panorama of bright colours and flashing lights. From this high vantage point, he was awestruck by the size of the metropolis. Its pulsing energy could be felt even in the sky.

As the plane got closer to Nigeria's Murtala Muhammed International Airport, he felt a mix of excitement and worry. Recent travel warnings from Canada had cast a shadow of worry over his mind, making him worry about his own safety and the fact that Canada's security situation was hard to predict. Terrorism, crime, fights between groups, armed attacks, and kidnappings were always on his mind.

He got caught up in a web of thoughts when he thought about the strong warnings against travelling to Nigeria for non-essential reasons, especially to Abuja. The advisory pointed out the dangers in certain areas and told travellers to stay away from the north-west, north-central, and north-eastern parts of the country, as well as the Niger Delta. These places were known for having a high risk of terrorism, armed attacks, kidnappings, and violence between different groups.

Also, the advisory shed light on the problems that Nigerian banks and ATMs are facing because of a chronic lack of cash caused by the release of new Naira notes. As a result of this lack of money, there were more violent acts, roadblocks, and attacks on ATMs and banks. This made Mark even more worried about financial transactions. He thought about the best thing to do and wondered if he should even go into a bank or use an ATM while he was there.

His worry was made worse by the recent presidential and gubernatorial elections, which were marked by political tensions and random acts of violence. He was very aware that the sounds of protests after the election could still be heard in the streets. To stay safe, he had to be very careful and follow the rules of the area.

The advisory went on to describe in detail the security risks in different parts of Nigeria. Terrorism, robbery, and kidnapping were scary possibilities in the northwestern and northeastern states. On the other hand, the Niger Delta states were involved in regional and ethnic wars, which led to violent crimes and civil unrest. Also, pirates were a constant threat in the coastal waters of the Niger Delta.

EIGHTEEN

As the plane gently descended towards the Muritala Muhammed International Airport in Lagos, Mark's excitement was palpable. He turned to the passenger sitting next to him, a friendly person named Kayode, and struck up a conversation.

"So, Kayode, can you feel the magic that's coming?" Mark asked with a gleam in his eyes, referring to the feeling of visiting Nigeria for the first time.

He smiled warmly, sharing his excitement, but there was a hint of curiosity in his expression. "I can sense your enthusiasm, but I'm curious, what brings a white man like you to Nigeria?"

He chuckled and replied, "Well, my friend, I was invited by a dear friend who lives here. I've heard so much about Nigeria's beauty and culture that I couldn't resist experiencing it firsthand."

He nodded, intrigued. "That's interesting. It's always nice to visit a place with a local guide, especially when it's a friend who knows the ins and outs."

As the plane continued its descent, Mark noticed Emeka, who had returned to his seat a few rows down. He waved at him, and he returned the wave with a warm smile. He turned back to Kayode and said, "Speaking of local guides, Emeka was telling me about some fantastic places to visit in Lagos."

Kayode looked interested. "Oh, really? That's great! Having someone who knows the city well can really enhance your travel experience."

Their talk soon shifted to the recent elections and the political tensions that followed. Mark brought up the importance of staying cautious during such times. "One needs to be careful and avoid crowded places, especially when there's political unrest," he advised.

Kayode gave a serious nod. "Protests after an election can have a long-lasting effect. It is very important to follow local rules and stay informed about the current situation."

As the plane prepared for landing, Mark couldn't help but think about the travel warnings he had read before coming to Nigeria. He had been warned about potential risks and unknowns, but his friend Arinze had reassured him over the phone that he would do everything to ensure his safety during his stay.

He shared his thoughts with Kayode, saying, "I was a bit concerned after reading the travel warnings, but my friend has been so supportive and assured me that he will take care of everything. It makes me feel better about the trip."

He smiled reassuringly. "Having a local friend looking out for you is a great advantage. I'm sure your trip will be both fun and safe with Arinze by your side."

As the plane touched down in Lagos, he felt a mixture of excitement and relief. He was eager to embrace the adventures that awaited him in Nigeria, knowing that he had a friend like Arinze to show him the beauty and warmth of the country while also ensuring his safety. The journey ahead was promising, filled with new experiences and the joy of discovering a land he had longed to explore

As he walked up to the immigration counter, he met an immigration officer whose attitude was typical of the delays and problems that are common at Nigerian airports. Their conversation took a strange turn, which made him even more worried than he was before.

"Anything for me?" the immigration officer asked in a local accent with a hint of amusement.

He wrinkled his brow, trying to figure out what the question meant. He replied politely, "I'm sorry, I didn't get it. Could you say that again?"

The officer's smile grew wider, and he looked like he was up to something. "You don't bring anything from America?" he asked, chuckling softly and speaking broken English.

He felt that the officer was making an assumption, so he said, "Oh, I see. No, I'm not from the United States. I'm coming all the way from Canada." He showed where his bag was. "And yes, I do have my personal belongings with me."

The immigration officer looked annoyed and could tell that other people in queue were getting impatient, so he reluctantly gave him his passport back. He told him to go away in a low voice, and he may have cursed under his breath.

His trip kept going, and as things happened, he was both surprised and confused. He couldn't understand why people would ask for favours or gifts in a place like an immigration office, which is a very formal place. The officer's rude behaviour made him wonder about their professionalism and the fairness of the system.

As he walked, his mind was full of thoughts. He thought about how to deal with rude or unprofessional airport workers. He didn't understand why visitors had to give something in exchange for things going more smoothly. It made people worry about who was responsible in the system.

He watched the National Drug Law Enforcement Agency officers do their searches and noticed that some of them were manually checking bags instead of using the right equipment to scan them. This made people question how well airport security works.

He thought about how Nigerian airports work in general because of the delays, rude staff, and strange things that happened there. He wanted things to get better, for people to be held more accountable, and for travellers to feel more welcome.

He started talking to a fellow traveller going in the same direction as him while he was on his way. Their talk gave them a chance to talk about their lives and worries.

"I can't believe what just happened over there. In such a formal setting, how could they ask for favours or gifts? "It makes no sense!" He exclaimed.

"Yes, you're right. It makes no sense at all. It makes you wonder about the officer's professionalism and the fairness of the system," the other passenger said.

Mark nodded in agreement. "Exactly! I've been wondering, "Is there a way to talk to airport workers about being rude or report their bad behaviour?"

The eyes of the other passenger lit up. "I thought the same thing. It's important to figure out how to make them answer for what they do. This sort of behaviour shouldn't be allowed."

He looked over at the NDLEA officers who were searching. "Have you also noticed that some officers were doing manual searches instead of using the right equipment for scanning? It worries me.

The other person sighed. "Absolutely. It makes people wonder if the security measures in place are really working. The most important thing should be our safety."

"All of these things have made me think about how Nigerian airports work as a whole. He said, "It's clear that the area needs to be improved and made more traveler-friendly."

The other passenger gave a firm nod. "I completely agree. Because of the delays, rude staff, and other problems, it's important to try to make the airport experience better. Travellers deserve better."

Their talk went up and down, and the words they said to each other showed that they had had similar experiences and were worried about similar things. It made people feel like they were all in it together and gave them hope that the airport system would get better.

As soon as he walked out of the arrival gate, he saw his friend Arinze waiting for him, which made him smile.

As soon as he saw Arinze at the airport arrivals, he felt a rush of happiness. Their warm embrace said a lot about how good their friendship was.

"It's great to see you, Arinze!" Mark yelled, smiling all the way up to his eyes. "Getting through the airport was a little hard, but I did it."

Arinze returned the hug, and his voice was full of genuine joy. "Hello, my friend! Welcome to Nigeria! I'm glad that you made it. How did your trip go?"

He let out a sigh as he thought about the good and bad parts of his trip. "Overall, it was fine, but there were some surprises during the immigration and security process. It kept me on my toes for sure."

Arinze nodded to show that he understood his feelings. "Ah, I understand. Sometimes it's hard to tell what will happen at an airport in Nigeria. My friend, don't worry. From now on, we'll make sure that the rest of your trip is fun and full of good memories."

He saw Arinze's sleek black SUV as they were walking to the parking lot. The car was in front of them, its polished surface shining in the sun. He couldn't help but be impressed by how clean it was and how sophisticated it looked.

"Wow, Arinze, your car is really impressive!" He shouted as he ran his hand over the smooth surface. "It looks like it's brand new."

As they settled into the luxurious cabin, Arinze laughed with a hint of pride in his voice. "Thank you, buddy. I just got it not long ago. I wanted to make sure you were happy while you were here. Now, get in the car, and let's go to my house. There's a lot to get up to speed on."

He looked around as they drove away from the airport. The air was hot and sticky, which is typical for Nigeria. They drove through busy streets that were full of bright colours, street vendors, and active people going about their daily lives. The air was full of the sounds of cars honking and people talking.

He looked out the window and saw that the buildings along the way were a unique mix of old and new. He couldn't help but notice the busy markets and small shops on the side of the road selling a wide range of goods, which added to the lively atmosphere.

Arinze leaned forward, and his eyes showed that he was interested. "So, Mark, how was the rest of your time at the airport? Is there anything else important?"

He took a moment to think about the time he had spent getting around the airport. "Well, other than my first experiences with immigration and security, I couldn't help but notice that some parts of the airport looked a little worn. It made me wonder about the maintenance and standards in general."

He nodded sympathetically because he agreed with what Mark said. He knew that Nigerian airports could have different kinds of buildings and service. But he kept looking at things in a positive way.

"Yes, you're right," said Arinze. "There are ways to make our airports better. It's still being worked on. But, you know, even with our flaws, this place has its own special charm."

He couldn't help but smile when he saw how positive he was. He knew that if he wanted to be a part of the Nigerian charm, he had to accept the challenges and differences that came with it.

Mark said, "Absolutely," and his excitement grew. "I'm here to fully embrace the charm of Nigeria and get involved in everything it has to offer. I'm ready for the exciting things and special moments that are waiting for me."

As they kept going, they talked in a way that was full of laughter and excitement. As they got closer to his neighbourhood, a suburban area with neatly lined houses and lots of greenery, Mark couldn't help but feel excited.

NINETEEN

The weather stayed warm, and the sun made everything look like it was made of gold. As they drove through the quiet streets, the smell of tropical plants filled the air, making it feel fresh.

He was getting more and more interested as they got closer to Arinze's house. He couldn't wait to learn about Nigerian culture and enjoy his hospitality.

He looked at him with a smile on his lips and an eager look in his eyes. "Arinze, I can already tell that this trip is going to be something special. "Thank you for being both my guide and my dear friend," he said with thanks.

Arinze's face lit up with a big smile, and his eyes sparkled with joy. "You're most welcome, my friend," he said with a smile. "Get ready for an amazing adventure in Nigeria, because we're just getting started."

When they got to his home in Ikeja GRA, a wealthy neighbourhood in Lagos, He couldn't help but be impressed by how grand everything was.

The richness of the neighbourhood was shown by the lush greenery in the streets and the beautiful houses. The beautiful duplex house that Arinze lived in was a mix of modern and Nigerian architecture. The outside was painted a warm beige colour, and big windows let lots of natural light into the house. The charm was added by a well-kept garden with bright flowers and neatly trimmed hedges.

As they approached the front door, Mark's anticipation grew, looking forward to meeting Arinze's wife, "NK" as their friends fondly called her. He remembered the times they had all spent together in Toronto, working together to support the Nigerian diaspora community.

The door swung open, revealing NK, a stunning woman with a bright smile that instantly lit up the room. Her vibrant Ankara print dress beautifully showcased Nigeria's rich cultural heritage, and her graceful, confident movements exuded a flawless sense of style. Her warm, welcoming personality immediately put Mark at ease.

"Mark! It's great to see you again. Welcome to our humble home!" NK greeted him with genuine joy.

His face lit up with a big smile as he replied, "NK, it's my pleasure. Thank you so much for being so kind and inviting me to stay with you."

Inside the house, the joyful shouts of their children greeted his arrival. The kids rushed towards him, calling out, "Uncle Mark!" and engulfed him in tight hugs, their laughter filling the air.

Amidst the commotion, Arinze's warm voice rang out, capturing the children's attention. "Kids, gather around! Uncle Mark is a dear friend from Toronto. Show him your love!" He beamed with pride, looking at his children fondly.

"Do you remember Uncle Mark?" Arinze asked, looking at his kids with a playful smile.

"Yes! He taught us how to make funny faces!" one of the children exclaimed, causing everyone to laugh.

"That's right!" Mark chimed in, joining the playful banter. "And you all are experts now, I'm sure!"

The children giggled and nodded in agreement, showcasing their best funny faces, which brought even more laughter to the room.

He followed them into the living room, where tasteful furnishings and a welcoming atmosphere greeted him. The vibrant throw pillows added splashes of color, complementing the comfortable furniture. Framed photographs adorned the walls, capturing cherished family memories and infusing the space with warmth and familiarity.

He guided him to the guest room, a tranquil haven prepared with care. The room exuded a sense of hospitality, adorned with tasteful decor and a bed dressed in crisp, clean sheets. Arinze pointed to the room, a friendly smile lighting up his face.

"Mark, this is your guest room," he conveyed with genuine warmth. "We've made sure it's a safe and comfortable space for you. Please feel free to settle in."

His's eyes wandered around the room, taking in the thoughtful touches awaiting him. Overwhelmed by their efforts to make him feel welcome, gratitude welled up within him. The soft lighting, the gentle sway of curtains in the breeze, and the inviting armchair beckoning him to relax all contributed to a profound sense of peace.

With a nod of appreciation, he stepped into the room. For a brief moment, the embracing warmth of this thoughtful space lifted the weariness of his long journey. As he sank into the plush armchair, a profound sense of gratitude washed over him, accompanied by a deep appreciation for his friend kindness and thoughtfulness.

"Thank you, both. This room is beyond what I could have imagined. You've truly made me feel welcome," Mark expressed sincerely.

"It's my pleasure, Mark. We wanted to ensure you have a comfortable and enjoyable stay. You're like family to us," Arinze replied warmly.

"I can't express how grateful I am for your hospitality. It means a lot to me," he confessed, his voice filled with genuine appreciation.

"You're part of our family, Mark. We're thrilled to have you here. Make yourself at home," she reassured him with a heartfelt smile.

His gratitude overflowed. "Thank you. I'm looking forward to spending quality time with all of you. It's been too long."

Their heartfelt conversation resonated with warmth and appreciation, further solidifying the bond them in this haven of love and care. At that moment, he knew that his time at his house was going to be very special. And as he made himself at home in the cosy guest room, he looked forward with excitement to the adventures and memories he would have on this exciting trip through Nigeria.

He turned to his hosts with a genuine smile on his face and said, "Thank you once again." "I can't thank you enough for the wonderful way you have treated me. This place really does feel like a home away from home.

They looked at each other, and their eyes showed how happy they were. They knew that their efforts to make the space friendly had paid off, and his appreciations made them feel good.

"Indeed, it's our pleasure to have you here," said Arinze in a sincere way. We want you to feel completely at ease and enjoy the warmth of our home."

His wife nodded in agreement, and her voice was full of real kindness. "Absolutely, Mark. We always have our doors and hearts open for you. It's great that you're here with us."

Sitting in the warm, comfortable home of his dear friends, He felt an overwhelming sense of gratitude for their true friendship and the safe haven they provided him. It was evident how close they were and how many cherished memories they had created together over the years. With a grateful heart, he looked forward to embarking on an unforgettable journey within Nigeria, alongside his best friend.

The long flight had left him feeling weary, but a refreshing shower washed away the tiredness, leaving him invigorated and ready to embrace the Nigerian experience. As he stepped out of the bathroom, the aroma of delectable dishes filled the air, making his mouth water. They had prepared a delightful spread, showcasing the rich and diverse flavors of Nigerian cuisine.

Sitting around the table with the family, Mark's taste buds danced with joy as he savored the jollof rice, juicy grilled chicken, and an array of traditional side dishes. The skillful blend of spices and careful cooking truly captured the essence of Nigerian food.

"Wow, everyone, this food is simply incredible! You've truly surpassed all expectations. I can hardly believe the amazing blend of flavors I'm experiencing," he exclaimed enthusiastically as he savored each bite. His genuine appreciation shone through his words, a testament to the exceptional effort that had gone into preparing the meal.

With each mouthful, he found himself more immersed in the symphony of tastes that danced across his palate.

The culinary masterpiece before him was a work of art, a creation that showcased not only culinary skill but a deep understanding of ingredients and their potential. As the conversation continued to flow around the table, his focus remained on the plate in front of him, his senses fully engaged in the sensory journey that was unfolding.

The family beamed with pride, delighted to see their guest thoroughly enjoying the labor of their love in the kitchen.

After a satisfying meal, Arinze suggested they venture to Surulere, a vibrant neighborhood in the heart of Lagos known for its bustling streets and lively atmosphere. He enthusiastically agreed, eager to explore more of the city.

TWENTY

Driving through the streets of Surulere, he was in awe of the vibrant shops, bustling markets, and the electrifying energy that permeated the air. The streets were alive with the sounds of laughter, music, and spirited conversations, painting a vivid picture of city life in Nigeria.

"Surulere is even livelier than I imagined! It's a perfect representation of the energetic spirit of Lagos," he remarked, admiring the bustling surroundings.

He grinned. "Yes, Lagos is a city that never sleeps. There's always something happening here, and you'll love every bit of it."

As they drove through the busy streets of the city, he got more and more excited. The grandeur of the National Stadium stood in front of them. Its height was awe-inspiring and showed how much Nigerians loved sports. It was in the middle of Lagos and stood as a sign of the city's active sports culture.

He drove the car through the stadium's gates and skillfully turned it towards the stadium complex, which was full of people and activities. When they got there, they found a hidden gem: Ojez, a famous restaurant that not only locals but also Nollywood actors and other well-known people like to go to.

They parked their car and walked towards Ojez. As they walked, they moved into a world of great food and cultural significance. The restaurant's doors opened, making them feel like they were invited to join the shared experiences and interesting conversations that had been going on inside.

When they walked into Ojez, they were greeted by a warm and lively atmosphere. In every corner of the restaurant, lively conversations and the rhythmic melodies of Nigerian music filled the air with a pleasant buzz. It was a great mix of different cultures and friendship.

As they settled into a cozy corner, the tantalizing aroma of grilled fish and suya filled the air, making their mouths water with anticipation. The speakers resonated with the soulful melody of an iconic song by a well-known Igbo musician. The powerful message of unity and togetherness in the song filled the room, creating an atmosphere of friendship.

He couldn't resist the urge to sing along, his voice exuding passion and emotion that the lyrics carried. Mark listened intently, even though he couldn't understand the words, captivated by the beauty of the melody and the emotions conveyed.

Curiosity got the better of him, and He leaned in, asking Arinze, "this song seems so powerful and meaningful. Could you tell me more about its significance in Igbo culture?"

His eyes lit up with enthusiasm at his genuine interest. "Absolutely, my friend. This song is called 'Onyeoma,' written by one of the most respected Igbo musicians of all time. It embodies the spirit of unity and showcases the strength that comes when we stand together. It touches upon the core values of our culture, emphasizing the importance of harmony and unity among our people."

His appreciation for the music deepened as Arinze shared the song's meaning. The vibrant atmosphere of Surulere, the iconic National Stadium, and the charming ambiance of Ojez blended together, painting a vivid picture of Nigerian culture.

Three of his friends joined them at Ojez, the atmosphere grew even livelier with the joyous reunion of friends. Arinze took a moment to introduce each of them to him, emphasizing the close bond they shared.

"Mark, I want you to meet my friends, Chinedu, Hassan, and Ade. These guys are like brothers to me. We share a passion for football and Nollywood movies, and most importantly, a common vision for a better Nigeria," he said with pride.

He greeted them warmly, shaking each of their hands. "It's a pleasure to meet all of you. Arinze has spoken highly of your friendship and the shared interests we have. I'm grateful to be a part of this amazing group."

Chinedu was a huge fan of football, and he couldn't hold back his excitement as he started a conversation about the sport, they all loved. "Mark, let me tell you that the Igbo local league in the South East has produced some amazing players. We need to put money into our clubs and help football grow at the local level. It's the key that will let us reach our full potential."

Hassan, whose eyes twinkled with mischief, said, "Well, Chinedu, you can't deny that our Hausa players are talented and determined. They are very fast and strong, which makes them hard to beat on national and international stages."

Ade added, with pride in his voice, "Guys, we shouldn't forget how much Yoruba athletes have done for Nigerian football. We've had some really great players, and our cultural knowledge gives us a unique edge on the pitch."

Mark was drawn in by their passionate conversation, so he told them what he thought. "It's interesting to hear what you have to say. Football really brings us all together, and it's amazing to see how talented people from all over Nigeria are. Through these talks, you can bring people together and build a better future for your beloved country.

As the night went on, they talked quickly, laughed, and talked about the good old days. The things that were talked about ranged from the state of Nigerian football to how Nollywood affects how films show Nigerian culture. Each person's voice fit well with the others', creating a symphony of ideas that helped them understand and appreciate their common goals.

In the lively ambiance of Ojez, their gathering radiated with warmth. The cheerful clinking of glasses, infectious laughter, and the seamless flow of conversation painted a vibrant portrait of friendship and the power of shared interests.

As the evening deepened, the dialogue naturally gravitated towards Nigeria's recent election, a topic rife with concerns about corruption within the Independent National Electoral Commission (INEC) and the pressing need for a transparent voting process.

Chinedu leaned in, his tone earnest as he remarked, "When we consider INEC's role in the election, it's hard to shake off the feeling that something's amiss. Peter Obi's case comes to mind."

Ade nodded thoughtfully, his brow furrowing. "Absolutely. The fairness of the process is questionable. It's as if there are hidden strings pulling the outcomes, regardless of the candidates' merits."

Hassan joined the conversation, his voice measured, "Yet, let's not overlook Tinubu, the 'Jagaban.' His political prowess and popularity positioned him as a strong contender."

Chinedu's eyes gleamed with conviction. "No doubt, Tinubu has a significant presence. But remember, a democracy thrives on a spectrum of voices and choices."

Ade's grin was accompanied by a raised glass, a silent salute. "Indeed, my friends. These discussions mirror the very essence of democracy."

Amidst the engaging banter, Ade shifted his gaze and added, "Speaking of choices, what about Atiku? His experience and North-origin certainly make him a noteworthy contender."

Chinedu nodded, acknowledging the point. "True, Atiku's candidacy holds its own weight. It's fascinating how each candidate brings a unique perspective to the table."

The argument got more heated as the tensions rose. Arinze spoke up when he saw that their friendship was getting strained. He did so in a calm and collected way, hoping to bring them back together. "My friends," he said in a soft voice, "let's not forget that these problems have been given to the Presidential Election Petition Tribunal to solve." Their job is to find out what happened and decide what happened. Until then, let's stop arguing about who won and who lost."

The group agreed with what he said, and they reluctantly stopped arguing about the controversial political topic. Knowing that these kinds of talks could hurt their relationship, Arinze skillfully changed the subject to something lighter and more neutral. This gave them a chance to switch gears and have a more fun conversation.

Again, there was laughter in the air as they told stories, talked about their favourite films, and joked about important times in their lives. The heated political talk faded into the background because they valued their friendship more than anything else.

In the safe place of Ojez, they kept talking about their shared experiences, ideas, and hopes. The night went on with laughter and goodwill, leaving a lasting impression of a group that celebrated friendship and the power of polite conversation.

"So," Arinze said with a smile, "have you all heard about the music festival that's going to happen in our city next month?" I've heard that both local and international artists will put on great shows. Mark, our guest, would enjoy the lively music scene here, we're sure. How do you feel?"

His plan to get people to talk about something else worked, as his friends jumped at the chance to talk about the new topic. The mood got better, and his friends started talking about music, artists, and how much fun it is to see live performances.

Arinze secretly let out a sigh of relief. He was glad that their friendship had stayed the same. He thought that their friendship was a special thing that shouldn't be ruined by political fights or different ideas. He had kept them away from the dangerous topic of politics with tact and care, making sure that their time together would be peaceful and fun for everyone.

As they talked about music, Mark, the guest, had listened carefully, his eyes shining with excitement. Arinze smiled, happy in the knowledge that he had made a place where friendships could grow, where people could talk about different things, and where their bond would not be broken.

In the lively ambiance of Ojez pub and grill, the friends engaged in a heartfelt conversation about the issue of tribalism towards the Igbo people in Nigeria. The topic weighed heavily on their minds, sparking a mix of frustration and sadness over the persistent divide faced by their fellow citizens.

Chinedu's voice trembled with emotion as he shared, "It's truly painful to witness the ongoing tribalism against the Igbo community within our own nation. Every one of us deserves equal opportunities and respect. It's disheartening that tribalism continues to cast its shadow."

Ade's tone held determination as he added, "You're absolutely right, Chinedu. We need to tear down these walls of prejudice and advocate for justice. Nigeria must evolve into a place where fairness and dignity prevail for all."

Mark listened intently and offered his perspective, saying, "It's truly saddening to hear that such tribalism persists. In my own country, I've witnessed marginalized groups fighting for their rights as well. The struggle for equality and mutual understanding knows no borders."

Amidst their fervent discussion, Ojez pub and grill bustled with activity. The attentive waitstaff moved gracefully, ensuring patrons enjoyed delectable dishes and overflowing glasses. Scents of tantalizing cuisine mingled with the sounds of laughter and impassioned conversations, creating an inviting and intellectually stimulating ambiance.

Enhanced by cultural artifacts and stunning Nigerian artwork, the rhythmic melodies of Nigerian music permeated the air, infusing their dialogue with the vibrant essence of their nation's soul.

As the night advanced, the friends delved deeper into the intricate tapestry of Nigeria's culture. They shared anecdotes, dispelled myths, and celebrated the unifying threads that bonded them as a closely-knit group.

Chinedu's warm smile accompanied a cherished memory from his childhood, "I often recall my grandmother's stories, passed down through generations. They served to connect us to our roots and filled us with a profound sense of pride in our heritage. Preserving our cultural legacy remains vital."

Arinze chimed in, his voice thoughtful, "You're both right in addressing the issue of tribalism. It's a deeply rooted problem that affects so many aspects of our society."

However, Hassan gently disagreed, "Arinze, while tribalism is a critical issue, I believe the core problem isn't just about how different tribes are treated. It's that the political and economic elite treat all citizens as second-hand. The masses face neglect, regardless of their tribe."

Mark nodded in agreement, "Hassan, you make a valid point. Until the masses unite to demand better governance and equal opportunities, the issue won't truly be resolved."

As the evening drew to a close, the friends bid each other farewell, hearts brimming with a renewed sense of unity and optimism. Ojez pub and grill had provided a nurturing space for them to engage in profound conversations that bridged differences and kindled a hopeful outlook for a brighter tomorrow.

TWENTY-ONE

They went on an adventure through the busy city of Lagos. He was excited to see its many different places and learn about its rich culture. As they got closer to the city's centre, Arinze talked with him to explain some of the places as they drove through the busy streets.

Their first stop led them to the renowned National Theatre, an embodiment of artistic brilliance. As they stepped inside the grand edifice, a wave of emotions swept over Mark—longing mingled with a tinge of melancholy. The corridors reverberated with echoes of past performances, evoking contemplation about the untapped potential residing within its walls.

Arinze, forever the optimist, leaned closer and whispered, his voice carrying a dream-like quality, "Just imagine, my friend, if this theatre could reclaim its former glory. Within these very walls lie the aspirations and visions of an entire nation, as well as artists from every corner of the globe."

He nodded in agreement, his gaze wandering through the vast expanse of the theatre. "Indeed, Arinze. The National Theatre stands as a symbol of what could be—a beacon of artistic renaissance that could inspire generations to come."

He nodded, and his mind was full of ideas. "It's a sign of how strong the people of Nigeria are. Even though there are problems, creativity and artistic pursuits continue to grow. Maybe one day this theatre will shine like it used to."

The next place they went was the beautiful Lekki Conservation Centre, where they walked along Africa's longest canopy walkway, which was very exciting. Mark's heart grew full of wonder as they walked through the lush canopy, surrounded by the symphony of birdsong and the soft rustling of leaves.

Arinze laughed when he saw how amazed Mark looked. "Doesn't nature have a way of making us feel small? Even in the busy city of Lagos, she reminds us of how life is a delicate balance and how beautiful the world is.

He nodded, and his eyes followed a baboon as it swung gracefully through the trees. "Absolutely, Arinze. It's really amazing how urban growth and the protection of natural spaces can go together so well. Every turn in Lagos brings a new surprise."

Their conversations and explorations went hand in hand, and each new thing they saw made them appreciate the city and its natural beauty in new ways. Lagos, with its different landscapes and lively atmosphere, became a place for him to learn about art, nature, and what it means to be Nigerian. Together, they enjoyed the city's energy and diversity, savouring the unplanned moments that happened and making memories that would shape their relationship with this exciting city for the rest of their lives.

Their next trip took them to Badagry, a town with a long history and a sad story about the slave trade. As they walked through the cobblestone streets, the voices of the past came back to them, telling stories of hardship and survival. He felt a deep weight in his chest. He was deeply moved by how heavy history was.

His voice turned sad as he shared stories of bravery and survival. "Mark, here in Badagry, we're facing the sad things that happened in our past. It's our job to remember and work hard to stop such bad things from happening again."

He couldn't look away from the Door of No Return, a reminder of all the people taken from their homes who would never come back. Feeling the weight of history, he made up his mind: he would stand up for fairness and doing what's right.

In the midst of their adventures, they enjoyed Nigerian snack, filled with tempting flavors. The smells of akara and puff-puff made their mouths water and sparked eating adventure.

Every bite made him happy, the different flavors and textures dancing on his taste buds. With each dish, he learned a story and understood better how Nigerian cooking fit into the country's culture.

He explained what each dish meant; his eyes proud. "This is akara, made from black-eyed peas. It shows how clever our people are, finding food even when things are tough. And here, we have dodo – fried plantains – which gives you a real taste of our beautiful land."

He grinned, caught up in the moment. "It's amazing how food can tell stories. Akara is about not giving up, and dodo is like a piece of our land on a plate. This is helping me connect with Nigeria even more."

He nodded, pleased. "You've got it, Mark. Food links us to our past, reminding us of where we come from and what we've been through."

He listened carefully because he was interested. "What's up with this golden puff-puff? It's very fluffy and light, and full of sweet flavours."

Arinze laughed; his voice full of love for the food of his country. "Puff, puff! It's a snack that people love and eat on special occasions. It stands for all the happiness and celebration in our lives."

As they tried more snacks and talked about family recipes, regional specialties, and the role of food in Nigerian culture, they were able to have deeper conversations. Each bite became an invitation to unravel the threads that linked traditions, heritage, and the collective memory of a nation.

Their sightseeing journey took them to the amazing town of Makoko, which was perched on the edge of the water and full of people who were strong even when things were hard. As their boat wound through the crowded waterways, his heart filled with a mix of feelings: admiration for the community's resourcefulness, humility in the face of overwhelming problems, and gratitude for the simple joys that brightened their lives.

Arinze leaned in close to him and whispered in a reverent tone, "This community is a sign of how strong the human spirit is. Even when things are hard, they find beauty, and their strength is an example to us all."

His eyes filled with tears as he looked at the beautiful scene in front of him: the colourful houses in Makoko, the infectious laughter of children playing, and the strong ties of a close-knit community. At that moment, he swore to himself that he would always remember to be humble and thankful.

Without going to one of Lagos's busy markets, their trip to the city would not be complete. He was caught up in a whirlwind of bright colours and lively conversation. Balogun Market was full of different voices and the sounds of things being moved around.

His laughter bubbled forth as he noticed his friend's keen interest in the array of textiles and intricate handicrafts. "Step into Lagos's vibrant business hub, my friend. This place embodies the entrepreneurial spirit that thrives within everyone."

Drawn by curiosity, his friend couldn't resist purchasing a few keepsakes to commemorate their journey. His hands traced the intricate patterns and diverse textures, forging a tactile connection with each piece. With every transaction, a bridge formed between buyer and seller. The market became a microcosm of Lagos – a mosaic of cultures, histories, and aspirations.

Engaging with local vendors amid the market's bustling energy, they delved into the origins of the crafts and the significance behind the items on display. Amidst laughter, haggling, and shared anecdotes, the market transformed into a vibrant tapestry, showcasing the spirited essence of Lagos.

Exiting the market, a sense of gratitude swelled within him for the myriad treasures that Lagos had bestowed upon them. Their journey was more than just a sightseeing venture; it had immersed him in the very fabric of Nigerian existence. His newfound appreciation for the city's resilience, creativity, and unity resonated deeply within his hearts.

His eyes lit up as he admired a vibrant piece of fabric. "This is truly remarkable. The craftsmanship here is a testament to the rich cultural heritage of Lagos."

Arinze nodded, a smile playing on his lips. "Absolutely, Mark. Every piece tells a story, and each artisan's handiwork carries the soul of the city."

As they strolled further into the market, he couldn't help but strike up a conversation with a vendor showcasing intricate beadwork. "Tell me about these stunning bead necklaces. They're so intricate."

The vendor beamed, clearly delighted to share. "These beads are part of our tradition, passed down through generations. They represent different aspects of life – unity, family, love. Each piece is carefully crafted to honor our heritage."

He turned to Arinze, awe in his voice. "It's incredible how these items hold so much meaning and history."

He nodded, his tone earnest. "Indeed, Mark. Every thread, every bead, weaves the story of Lagos's people and their journey."

As they concluded their visit to the market, he gazed around, taking in the hurried scene. "This experience has opened my eyes to the heart and soul of Lagos."

He clapped Mark on the back. "And that, my friend, is the true essence of travel – not just witnessing, but immersing ourselves in the beauty and vitality of another culture."

With hearts full of newfound appreciation, they continued their journey, the vibrant echoes of the market's liveliness resonating within them.

TWENTY-TWO

They were tired after a day of exploring and adventure, so they went to the peaceful Moist Beach Club to rest and unwind. When they sat down in the comfortable lounge chairs on the deck, the warm sun wrapped around them, inviting them to relax and enjoy the peace. The rhythmic crashing of the waves was a soothing sound that added to their feeling of peace.

He leaned back in his chair and smiled, happy with how things were going. "Times like these really help me understand how many opportunities Lagos gives its people. This city has a lot of natural beauty, a long history, lively markets, and quiet beaches that have captured my heart.

He nodded, and his eyes showed that he agreed. "Indeed, Mark. Lagos is a city full of contrasts and strange meetings. It forces us to question our beliefs, be strong, and look for beauty in the most unlikely places.

As the sun began to set and cast a golden glow over the city, his mind was full of thanks. He would never forget the people he met, the things he did, or the friends he made during his time in Lagos. What started out as a trip to learn more about lagos had turned into a deep connection to Nigeria's rich history, cultural traditions, and people's unbreakable spirit.

As the night went on, they had heartfelt conversations in which they talked about their favourite times, shared stories from their own lives, and thought about how much Lagos had changed their views. With each conversation, their bond grew stronger, and they began to feel more like family, proving the power of shared experiences.

Both men enjoyed the peaceful atmosphere of Moist Beach Club as the sun went down, painting the sky with pink and orange colours. He knew that his time in Lagos had given them a better understanding and appreciation of the city's lively spirit. And with thankful hearts, they took in the peace and harmony that washed over them. He will always remember how this trip through Lagos changed them.

Early on Sunday morning, he knocked on his door. When he got an answer, he walked in with a warm smile. "Greetings, Mark. Would you like to go to church with my family on Sunday?" he asked.

He was happy to be asked, so he nodded and said, "Yes. I'd be happy to go to church with you and your family."

He has always been a Christian. His parents taught him to believe in God, but he hasn't been to church in a long time. He saw this as a chance to get back in touch with his faith and worship in a different way.

Together with his host family, they all went to the church where Arinze was an active member, St. Paul Anglican Church. As soon as they walked into the church, the ushers and churchgoers greeted him warmly, making him feel right at home.

Inside the church, there were beautiful stained-glass windows that showed scenes from the Bible. The pews were full of people who wanted to worship, and the lively Nigerian choir led them in singing beautiful hymns.

He was amazed by how devoted and passionate the worshippers were. He saw that the church was packed, which was different from what he had seen in Canadian churches, where attendance was often low.

At the end of the service, they left the church, their spirits were uplifted by the powerful sermon they had just heard. He couldn't contain his excitement as he turned to Arinze, a smile lighting up his face. "Arinze, that sermon really struck a chord with me. The Reverend's words about love, unity, and living out our faith resonated so deeply. It's a reminder of how important it is to align our actions with our beliefs."

He nodded in agreement, his eyes reflecting a sense of conviction. "Absolutely, Mark. It's easy to get caught up in the routines of life, but moments like this remind us of the core values that should guide us. I feel inspired to make a greater effort to live out my faith and spread love and unity wherever I go."

As they made their way through the church courtyard, he introduced him to some of the congregants. The warm greetings and genuine smiles warmed his heart, affirming the sense of community he had felt during the service. One of the parishioners, Mrs. Johnson, approached them with open arms. "Welcome, Mark! We're so glad you could join us today. The church is a place of love and acceptance, and we hope you felt that here."

He returned her embrace, a genuine gratitude shining in his eyes. "Thank you, Ma'am. I truly felt the warmth and love in this church. It's inspiring to witness such a tight-knit community, bound together by their faith."

As they stepped out into the lively streets of Lagos, his gaze fell upon the myriad places of worship that adorned the cityscape. He couldn't help but express his amazement. "Arinze, it's incredible to see how deeply rooted religion is in Nigeria. The sheer number of churches and mosques is a testament to the faith and spirituality of the people. It's a beautiful reflection of the diverse fabric of this country."

He nodded, his eyes filled with a mix of pride and contemplation. "You're right, Mark. Nigeria is a place where different religious beliefs coexist harmoniously. It's a reminder that regardless of our individual faiths, we all share a common humanity and a desire for peace and unity."

As they drove home along the less busy streets, his thoughts turned to the paradoxical nature of faith and its impact on society. "Arinze, it's interesting how religion, which is meant to inspire goodness and moral values, can sometimes be overshadowed by corruption and societal challenges. It makes me wonder how people can claim to be religious yet engage in unethical practices."

A touch of solemnity settled over him, his voice carrying a gentle undercurrent of sadness. "Mark, I can appreciate your concern. The truth is, no religious community is entirely immune to challenges. Yet, it's crucial to understand that faith is deeply personal. Each individual shapes their beliefs according to their understanding. We should prioritize our actions, serving as living examples of authenticity and integrity."

Their dialogue took on a contemplative hue as Mark, his gaze warm, expressed his heartfelt admiration for Arinze's inherent kindness and unswerving honesty. "Arinze, the way you live your life is a true embodiment of faith. Your character radiates the transformative power that strong beliefs can have on a person. You inspire me to strive for personal growth."

His smile blossomed, his humility endearing. "Thank you, Mark. However, it's essential to remember that each of us is on a distinct spiritual journey. We can learn from one another, enriching our perspectives. Our conversations and shared experiences become the building blocks of our faith and the shaping of our character."

As their thoughtful conversation continued, the journey home unfolded around them. The streets of Lagos were bustling with life, a vibrant backdrop to their contemplation. In the back seat, his children were engaged in a game, their laughter weaving a cheerful thread through the discourse. Every now and then, they would glance out of the window, captivated by the play of sunlight on the cityscape.

The weather, a mix of sunshine and fleeting clouds, seemed to mirror the ebb and flow of their conversation. Nkechi, Arinze's wife, chimed in, her voice gentle and wise. "Indeed, faith holds the potential to guide us towards positive transformations. It's a binding force that can bridge our differences."

He nodded, his gaze shifting between Arinze and Nkechi. "Nk, you bring such insightful perspectives to our talks."

He chuckled; his eyes affectionate as he glanced at his children in the rearview mirror. "Our little ones are enjoying the ride, too. Their laughter is a reminder of the simple joys that faith can bring."

She nodded, her eyes twinkling. "They remind us of the purity of belief that children possess. It's a beautiful thing to witness."

The journey continued, a harmonious blend of introspection and shared experiences. His thoughts wandered, contemplating the vast impact of spirituality on individuals and society. He couldn't help but muse aloud, "Imagine if the collective faith of Nigerians could drive the nation toward progress, justice, and kindness."

His voice held a note of optimism. "Indeed, Mark. It starts with individuals, like us, striving to embody the principles we hold dear. Our actions have a ripple effect."

Lost in their meaningful exchange, they continued their journey home. The streets of Lagos seemed to hum with a renewed sense of purpose as they contemplated the significance of faith.

As they kept driving, he couldn't help but think about how spirituality affects people and communities. He hoped that one day, the faith of all Nigerians would lead to positive changes that would move the country towards progress, justice, and kindness.

TWENTY-THREE

They ate Launch together as family, she started a conversation with him. Her warm smile let him know that she was happy to talk to him. She was interested in his personal life, so she asked him about it. "Mark, I remember that you were married when we were in Toronto. How are your kids and your wife?"

He replied, "Yes, Nk, I was married." There was a hint of sadness in his eyes. We ended up getting a divorce because my marriage didn't work out. We all had a hard time during that time."

He met her kind eyes, and she knew that what he said was important. "Mark, I'm sorry to hear that. Everyone can have a hard time during a divorce. How do you feel now?"

He took a moment to gather his thoughts before answering, "It's been a journey of self-reflection and growth for me. I've realised that my ego played a part in the end of my marriage, and I've been working hard to improve myself. My ex-wife has since gotten married again, which I've come to accept. What matters most to me right now is getting back in touch with my kids."

She nodded, and her face showed that she understood. "That's a good thing, Mark. It takes courage to recognise our flaws and try to improve ourselves. I'm glad to hear that you and your kids are getting closer again. Family is important, and it's never too late to make up with them and make their lives better.

His face got a little brighter as he went on. "Yes, you're right, Nk. I feel lucky to be able to be a part of my kids' lives again. It gives me a chance to be a better dad and make up for the time I missed. I promise to be there for them and build a relationship based on love and support."

He heard all the different feelings in the room and said something to help. "Mark, it's never easy, but it's important to forgive and grow. Keep your mind on the present and the future, and enjoy the time you spend with your kids. They will love you for all the work you do for them."

As the conversation went on, he felt better and was thankful that they understood and helped him. Even though the road to healing and making up with his children was still long, he was ready to take it on with an open heart and a willingness to make things right.

The two men left Lagos in the morning to go to his village in southeastern Nigeria, the air was full of excitement as they drove through the beautiful landscape on the winding roads, the beauty, and charm of the village that was waiting for them slowly came into view. Traditional huts with thatched roofs stood next to modern buildings, which showed that the village had a long history and was also open to change.

He pointed to the changing landscape with pride in his eyes. "Mark, can you see that our town is changing? Both at home and abroad, our people are making great progress and helping our community grow.

He couldn't help but be amazed by how alive the village was. It buzzed with an energy that couldn't be denied as if it had its own heartbeat. The combination of traditional and modern elements brought life to every corner. "Arinze, it's amazing to see how old and new fit together so well in your village. It really shows how strong and adaptable the people are."

When they got to the village, it was the New Yam Festival, which everyone was looking forward to. It was a happy time to celebrate the good harvest and give thanks for the year's blessings. As they watched the plans come together, the air was filled with excitement and anticipation. He was interested, and he couldn't wait to dive into the cultural extravaganza that was waiting for him.

His voice was full of excitement as he talked about how important the festival was. "Mark, the New Yam Festival is a time for big parties and giving thanks. It shows how important farming is and how much our people like to work together. Get ready to see how lively our traditions are."

As soon as the festival started, the village came to life with a mixture of activities, pulsing music, and rhythmic dance. The delicious smell of yam dishes filled the air, and laughter could be heard all over the village streets. He was filled with cultural pride as he watched the amazing show that was happening in front of him.

He turned to him with awe in his voice. "Arinze, I can't believe how united and friendly everyone is in the village right now. When everyone comes together to celebrate their shared heritage, it's inspiring to see how close the community is.

As Mark and Arinze stepped into the heart of the village, they were immediately swept up in the vibrant tapestry of the New Yam Festival. The air buzzed with energy as the rhythmic beats of drums echoed through the streets, and the villagers adorned in colorful traditional attire danced with unabashed enthusiasm.

Arinze's eyes glinted with pride as he turned to Mark, his voice filled with excitement. "Welcome to the New Yam Festival, my friend. This is a celebration of our culture, our unity, and our deep connection to the land."

Mark's gaze was captivated by the swirling colors and the palpable sense of joy that enveloped the scene. "It's truly a sight to behold, Arinze. The energy here is incredible."

As they continued to soak in the festivities, they were approached by a group of villagers led by an elder named Chukwuemeka. With an air of reverence, Chukwuemeka welcomed them warmly. "Greetings, Arinze! And who is this you've brought with you?" he inquired, his eyes falling on Mark.

Arinze grinned proudly. "Chukwuemeka, meet my friend Mark. He's come all the way from Canada to experience our beautiful festival."

Chukwuemeka's eyes crinkled in a welcoming smile as he extended his hand to Mark. "You are welcome, Mark, as an honored guest in our village. It warms our hearts to see people from different corners of the world embrace our traditions."

Mark shook Chukwuemeka's hand with genuine appreciation. "Thank you for having me. I'm honored to be here."

Arinze leaned in, his voice carrying a hint of nostalgia. "Mark, do you remember the times I used to tell you stories about my hometown while we were in Toronto? Well, here we are, experiencing it firsthand."

Mark chuckled, the memories resurfacing. "You always spoke of it with such passion. And now I can see why."

As the day progressed, Mark and Arinze found themselves in the presence of the Igwe, the village king. He exuded an air of wisdom and regality as he greeted them warmly. "Welcome, Arinze, and welcome to you, Mark. We are delighted to have you both join our celebration."

Arinze's eyes glowed with pride as he introduced Mark. "Igwe, this is my friend Mark. He's shown great interest in our culture and has traveled all this way to be part of the festival."

The Igwe's gaze settled on Mark, his eyes holding a depth of understanding. "Mark, we honor the spirit of unity and friendship that brings you here. You are now an honorary member of our community, and we bestow upon you the title of 'Nwanne Di Na Mba,' which translates to ' the brother from a foreign land.'"

Mark's heart swelled with gratitude, and he bowed respectfully. "I am truly humbled by your generosity, Igwe. Thank you for welcoming me with such open arms."

Arinze beamed at Mark, a sense of understanding between them. "Mark, it's surreal to think that we were friends in Toronto, and now you're here, embraced by my hometown in Nigeria."

Mark clapped Arinze on the shoulder, a genuine smile on his face. "Life has a way of weaving remarkable journeys, my friend. I'm grateful to be part of this one."

Upon the conferment of the title on Mark, the atmosphere became even more electrifying. The rhythmic beats of drums and the melodious tunes of flutes filled the air as the cultural dancers and musicians took center stage. Among them, a seasoned flutist began to play a soul-stirring melody, his music resonating with the hearts of the villagers.

In a mysterious and esoteric language known only to a few of the elder members, the flutist sang Mark's praises, invoking the blessings of the ancestors of Arinze's village. His flute seemed to carry messages to the heavens, a plea for Mark's safe journey back and the fulfillment of his goodwill.

As the song echoed through the gathering, the dancers and musicians joined in, their movements and voices harmonizing with the spirit of celebration. Arinze, with a mischievous smile, nudged Mark to join the dance. With a lighthearted chuckle, Mark surrendered to the rhythm, his steps a joyful echo of the village's ancient traditions.

Laughter erupted from the crowd as Mark attempted the dance, his earnestness more than making up for any missteps. The villagers appreciated his genuine participation, his willingness to embrace their culture with open arms.

Amidst the dance, Mark felt a strong connection to the moment—a bridge between his world and theirs, forged through dance and music. As the dance reached its crescendo, Arinze's infectious energy fueled their movements, and the applause from the villagers mingled with their laughter.

When the dance concluded, Mark stood before the Igwe once more, feeling the weight of the title and the warmth of the villagers' acceptance. With sincerity in his voice, Mark spoke, "I am grateful for this honor, Igwe. I promise to return to this land, to be part of the growth and prosperity of your community."

The crowd erupted in thunderous applause, their joy resonating throughout the village square. The Igwe's voice rose above the cheers, his words carrying the weight of tradition and the collective blessing of the villagers. "May your path be guided by the spirits of our ancestors, and may your journey be filled with peace."

Nze Okeke, a distinguished Ozo title holder, stepped forward. Holding a small gourd of nzu—white chalk—in his hand, he began to chant prayers in a mix of Igbo and English, his voice rising and falling like a sacred melody.

"Ọkwa nwanne di na mba, ka Chukwu si n'ihi na-akpotara n'anya," Nze Okeke intoned, his words carrying the weight of tradition.Meaning: "As the brother from a foreign land, may God watch over you wherever you go."

The villagers, their eyes closed in reverence, added their murmured "Amens" to Nze Okeke's prayers, their collective faith merging with the spiritual energy of the moment. The skies, which had been cloudy, seemed to part, allowing the sun's rays to bathe the village square in a golden glow—a sign, perhaps, of the ancestors' approval.

In that sacred convergence of dance, music, and prayers, Mark felt a profound sense of belonging and acceptance. His heart swelled with gratitude for the bonds he had forged in this village, and for the promise he had made to return as a beacon of hope and change.

As the day unfolded, they immersed themselves in the festivities, forging deeper connections with the villagers and experiencing the New Yam Festival in all its glory. The honor bestowed upon Mark by the Igwe and the friendship they shared with the villagers underscored the profound impact of their visit, a testament to the enduring power of friendship and the unifying thread of cultural heritage.

He looked at his friend with thanks in his eyes as the party was going on. "Arinze, this has been a truly life-changing event. At the New Yam Festival, I got to see for myself how rich and beautiful Nigerian culture is. I'm thankful for how warmly your community has welcomed me and for the chance to be a part of this celebration."

As he hugged his friend, his smile gave off a warm feeling. "Having you here has made us happy and strengthened our bonds. The New Yam Festival reminds us of how strong our traditions are and how hardy our people are. I'm glad you were able to see how beautiful our culture is."

His heart was full of memories and a deep appreciation for the village, its people, and the richness of their cultural heritage as the festival came to an end. The event had made him more open-minded and left an indelible mark on his soul.

He led him through the happy crowd and told him what the New Yam Festival was all about. "Mark, this festival is not just about celebrating the harvest," Arinze said. "It's a time for everyone in the community to get together and say thank you to the gods and ancestors who have given us so much. It's a party to celebrate what we've all done and how close we are."

He couldn't help but be drawn to the mesmerising masks at the festival, even though he was having a good time. Each masquerade had its own meaning, and the costumes were carefully made to represent different gods or ancestral spirits. As he focused the lens of his camera to capture the essence of the moment, he was amazed by the artistry and rich cultural heritage that were being shown.

He was really interested in the masquerade called "Ijele." It was very tall and looked powerful and mysterious with its bright feathers and intricate beadwork. Mark felt a mixture of excitement and awe when he saw how powerful Ijele was at the festival. Arinze said, "Ijele shows the strength and spirit of our community as a whole. It is a reminder of the help and protection our ancestors gave us."

In the village, he had the fortunate opportunity to meet Arinze's cherished grandmother. As they engaged in conversation, Arinze's translations lent a deeper understanding to their shared experiences. Mark and Arinze had both endured the loss of their parents, yet their paths of coping with grief diverged. While Mark had lost his parents at a tender age, Arinze's parents had passed away merely a few years back. Both losses were the inevitable result of the passage of time – his mother first, followed by his father a year later.

Despite most of their exchanges being conducted in Igbo, his adept translations bridged the gap, allowing Mark to grasp the profound closeness they shared. The elderly woman exuded wisdom and grace, her eyes reflecting a lifetime of lived experiences. He found himself enchanted by the melodious cadence of her words, which resonated like a cherished old hymn, echoing through the village.

His grandmother spoke with a voice that carried the weight of history and the tender affection of a grandmother. He listened intently, treasuring the rare privilege of immersing himself in the collective memories and profound wisdom of the village. Through Arinze's artful translations, her narratives unfurled like a vivid tapestry of cultural legacy, transmitting the age-old knowledge and invaluable lessons passed down by their ancestors.

He leaned forward; his curiosity evident. "Arinze, what is your grandmother sharing with us now?"

He smiled, translating the words with care. "She's telling us about the importance of community bonds in the face of adversity. She believes that the strength of a village lies in its unity."

He nodded thoughtfully. "It's incredible how these teachings are universal across cultures. Unity truly is a powerful force."

His grandmother's gaze shifted to Mark, a kind glint in her eyes. "She says that despite the differences in our backgrounds, our shared humanity connects us all."

He felt a warmth in his heart. "That's a beautiful sentiment."

As they continued to converse, he couldn't help but inquire, "Arinze, how did your grandmother learn all these stories?"

His translation carried a touch of reverence. "She says that these stories were passed down to her by her own grandparents. It's the way knowledge is preserved in our culture."

His gaze lingered on the elderly woman; admiration evident. "It's amazing how the wisdom of generations can live on through stories."

His grandmother leaned in, her eyes twinkling. Arinze translated with a chuckle, "She wants you to know that you're now a part of these stories too."

His heart swelled with gratitude. "I'm truly honored."

As their conversations flowed, he found himself becoming deeply enmeshed in the tapestry of the village's history and heritage. Through his translations, he uncovered a wellspring of profound insights and ageless wisdom that transcended language and culture. Their time with Arinze's grandmother became an enriching journey, a rare glimpse into the timeless essence of their shared humanity.

He was in awe of the people in the village because of how beautiful they were. The girls were beautiful and graceful, and their bright clothes showed how lively they were. He liked how their clothes seemed to move and dance with every step. He thought it was a beautiful way to celebrate life. Men were just as impressive, and their size and strength made them worthy of respect and admiration. Their hard work was shown by their calloused hands, which showed how tough and dedicated they were.

He looked at him with genuine awe as he took in the beauty of the village. "Arinze, the people in your village are really something special. The girls have such grace and style, and the men are like strong pillars. It's amazing to see how strong-willed and committed they are.

He was happy and proud, and his voice was full of love for his people. "Mark, our people are the most important part of our history. The beauty you see isn't just skin deep; it shows the strength, resilience, and rich cultural traditions that have been passed down from generation to generation.

As they talked, he got more and more interested in the village's stories and customs. He was amazed by how much thought went into their customs, how their values were woven into their daily lives, and how important it was to them to keep their cultural heritage alive.

As he told another story from the village, Arinze's eyes lit up with excitement. "Mark, let me tell you why our traditional dances are important. They tell the stories of our people and keep us connected to our ancestors. They are also a way to celebrate and express ourselves. During the festival, you'll see and hear the rhythms and movements that are so interesting."

He was getting more and more interested and excited. "Thank you, Arinze, for giving me the chance to learn about the deep and rich culture of your village. These times of understanding and connection are truly priceless.

When his grandmother saw how close Mark was to her grandson, she said something with a soft smile. "It makes me happy to see how our traditions continue to bring people from different cultures and generations together. Mark, remember these things and the lessons they teach you. The history of our village is kept alive by people like you who know how beautiful and important it is.

He nodded; his heart full of thanks. "Thank you, Granny . I'm grateful to have been invited into your village and to be able to learn from you all. Your knowledge and stories will always be special to me."

TWENTY-FOUR

As the first rays of the sun turned the sky a golden colour, He gently woke him up. His excitement was contagious. The air was full of a lively energy because everyone was looking forward to a day full of new discoveries. He told him where they were going with a sparkle in his eyes. He said that they were going to the busy village market, which is the heart of our village culture. His eyes lit up at the thought of joining in with all the fun.

"Mark, get up and be bright! We're going to the village market today, where you'll get a real taste of our market culture. It has many different colours, sounds, and tastes. "Get ready for a trip!" Arinze exclaimed.

He got up and followed his lead with a smile of eagerness on his face. Their steps fit in with the sounds of nature waking up, making a rhythm that matched the day's progress. As they got closer to the busy market, the quiet of the early morning gave way to a symphony of lively voices and busy movement.

"Arinze, I can feel the excitement and energy in the air. This market really does seem to be the heart of the village. he said, "I am curious."

Navigating the market's winding paths was an adventure in itself, with Mark skillfully following Arinze through the vibrant maze of stalls and sellers. As they entered the bustling market, the warm atmosphere embraced them, accompanied by the lively calls of market women and men.

"Welcome, Nwanne Di Na Mba!" some of the vendors called out with joyful smiles, acknowledging Mark's conferred title. Arinze chuckled and nudged Mark gently. "Remember, Mark, they are hailing you as the 'Brother from a Foreign Land.' It's an honor they're bestowing upon you."

Mark grinned, raising his hand in a friendly wave. "Thank you, everyone! It's truly an honor to be here among you all."

They soon stumbled upon a stand that still showcased yams from the recent New Yam Festival. Arinze engaged in a respectful and friendly conversation with the yam vendor, highlighting the significance of these yams to their community.

"Bros, these yams aren't just food. They carry the blessings of a bountiful harvest and unity among our people," Arinze explained, gesturing toward the intricate designs and vibrant colors adorning the yams.

Mark observed the scene with genuine interest, captivated by the strong bond between the community and their agricultural traditions. "It's incredible how deeply connected these yams are to the heart of this town," Mark remarked. "They're symbols of pride and unity."

Continuing their journey through the market, Arinze led Mark to a spot where palm wine flowed freely. As they approached a vendor offering the golden elixir in gourds, lively conversation and laughter filled the air.

"Ah, my friends, welcome to my humble corner of stories and tradition," the vendor proclaimed with a hearty smile. "Each gourd of palm wine holds the tales of our ancestors, stories that have traveled across generations. Allow me to share them with you."

Arinze and the vendor engaged in animated conversation, laughter echoing across the busy market. Mark leaned in, thoroughly absorbed in the storytelling and the vibrant atmosphere around him.

"Arinze, it's fascinating how stories are interwoven into every aspect here, even in the palm wine," Mark commented, his eyes reflecting appreciation. "It's a beautiful way to preserve the past and honor traditions."

Taking part in the ancient ritual of drinking palm wine, Mark felt a connection to the land and its stories. The experience was a bridge that linked him to the heart of the village.

"With each sip of palm wine, I'm tasting the essence of this land, the stories that have shaped it," Mark thought, his heart touched by the depth of history and culture.

Their market exploration continued, leading them to the meat section where the aroma of raw meat filled the air. Arinze's skillful bargaining and lively interactions with the meat sellers added to the festive ambiance.

"Mark, haggling here is more than just business—it's an art, a connection," Arinze exclaimed with enthusiasm. "It's about the camaraderie, the laughter, and the shared joy of being together."

As Mark observed the spirited negotiations and friendly banter, he couldn't help but be captivated by the sense of community that permeated the meat section.

"Arinze, it's remarkable how something as simple as food can create such a lively bond among people," Mark remarked, his eyes tracing the interactions around them. "This market is a celebration of culture, a place continued their exploration of the market, each moment deepening their understanding of Nigerian life and culture. The lively energy of the crowd, the array of colors, and the mingling of voices painted a vivid picture of a vibrant society united by the thread of tradition and community.

He smiled, and his eyes were full of pride. "You've got it just right." The market is the centre of our community and where our culture comes to life. It's a place where people tell stories, keep traditions alive, and make friends."

As they went deeper into the market, they saw a group of people pushing barrows. Their sweaty foreheads showed how hard they were working. Mark couldn't help but be attracted to how hard they worked. "Look at those people pushing wheel barrows. Their strength and resolve are amazing. "They carry more than just their own weight; they carry their families' hopes and dreams."

He nodded; his eyes full of respect. "You're right on the money, Mark. These people who push wheelbarrows show how strong our people are. They find strength in their family and community ties and help each other through the problems they face.

He walked up to one of the people pushing the wheelbarrows and started talking to them. "Excuse me, sir. I'm impressed by how strong and tough you are. How do you have the courage to carry such heavy loads day after day?"

The man who pulled the wheelbarrow smiled warmly at him. His face showed that he was determined and wise. "Ah, my friend, we have the strength to keep going because we love our families and know we are part of something bigger. We carry each other's burdens, which gives us comfort and strength."

He listened carefully, and his respect for what the wheelbarrow pusher said grew. "In fact, the real wealth in life is the bonds we make and the unity we work to build."

Arinze chimed in, nodding in agreement. "Absolutely." Our culture thrives because of these connections, which are built on resilience and kindness. The market is more than just a place to buy and sell things; it's a tapestry of people's lives and stories."

The man who pulled the wheelbarrow nodded, and you could see a bit of gratitude in his eyes. "You understand, my friends. In the hustle and bustle of this market, we celebrate the strength, kindness, and unity of our people."

Eventually they left the busy market with a better understanding of how Nigerian culture is all connected. He was thankful for the lessons they learned and the people they met. The vibrant tapestry of the market had left an indelible mark on his soul. It had given him a new sense of humility, gratitude, and a deep understanding of the true wealth that lies in the richness of human connections.

He felt enriched by the warm conversations and real connections he had with the villagers during their trip. He liked how they worked together and were determined to keep their traditions while also moving forward. The village had a unique feel because it was a mix of old and new, of tradition and change. This showed that the village could change without losing its core.

He was sad to leave the village, but he took with him a deep appreciation for the strong and united spirit that lived there. He was able to see the power of change in a community that was rooted in its history but also open to new things. It was a life-changing event that changed the way he thought about Nigerian culture and left an indelible mark on his journey of discovery and personal growth.

TWENTY-FIVE

Him and his friend, Arinze, had embarked on an extraordinary journey through Nigeria, soaking in the country's vibrant culture, breathtaking landscapes, and captivating traditions. Their adventure had taken them from the bustling streets of Lagos to the serene charm of a southeastern village, and now, to the lively heart of Calabar in the south-south. In each corner of Nigeria, they had woven a tapestry of indelible memories.

As they bid farewell to the village, the road led them to the enchanting city of Calabar. The city's vibrant energy was palpable, a dynamic fusion of modernity and tradition that exhilarated the air. Their trusted guide and friend, regaled him with tales that brought Calabar's extensive history and cultural richness to life.

Amidst the bustling markets, they both meandered through the aromatic maze of stalls. The kaleidoscope of scents and colors was a visual symphony, intensified by the animated exchanges of market vendors. The liveliness of the scene was as enchanting as it was immersive. His curiosity for Calabar's famed cuisine led him to eagerly sample the local delicacies.

Following Arinze, they arrived at a bustling food stand where the tantalizing aroma of Edikang Ikong filled the air. Mark's eyes sparkled with anticipation as he savored the first spoonful of the rich, verdant soup. A symphony of flavors danced on his taste buds – a harmonious blend of earthy vegetables and savory meats that left him craving more.

Arinze chuckled, his eyes brimming with pride. "Mark, you're truly savoring the essence of Calabar's cuisine. But remember, Edikang Ikong is just the beginning. These dishes are a reflection of our vibrant culture, a fusion of tastes and techniques passed down through generations."

Nodding in agreement, Mark continued relishing the delectable soup. "I'm grateful to you for introducing me to these extraordinary flavors. Each dish tells a story, connecting me to the people, traditions, and history of Calabar."

Their conversation delved beyond food – Mark learned about the renowned Calabar Carnival, a colorful extravaganza celebrating the city's rich cultural heritage. A sparkle of enthusiasm lit up Arinze's eyes as he spoke about the revelries of the carnival.

"Mark, you must experience the Calabar Carnival firsthand. It's an extraordinary showcase of our people's creativity, unity, and determination. While your visit won't coincide with the carnival, consider coming back in December to witness the vibrant streets and infectious joy," Arinze said with genuine excitement.

Mark's smile radiated enthusiasm. "I'm eagerly anticipating the chance to witness the Calabar Carnival myself. It's incredible how an event can beautifully highlight a city's history, traditions, and spirited essence. I'll definitely consider planning my visit around the carnival month, as you've suggested."

Their journey continued, with Mark and Arinze exploring the diverse at\tractions that Calabar had to offer. From historical landmarks to scenic wonders, the city showcased a harmonious blend of old and new, tradition and modernity.

In addition to their cultural explorations, lodging in Calabar was a delightful experience. The Transcorp Hotel Calabar, a favored choice, provided a luxurious haven.

Offering well-appointed rooms adorned with modern amenities, the hotel boasted sweeping views of the Calabar River. Impeccable hospitality services ensured a comfortable stay, while the tranquil ambiance added to its appeal. The hotel's elegantly designed spaces, including a swimming pool, fitness facilities, and a variety of dining options, catered to both leisure and business travelers.

Alternatively, the Marina Resort offered a unique accommodation experience, with charming chalets and cottages overlooking the picturesque Calabar River. Its prime location in close proximity to various attractions made it a desirable option for those seeking convenience and relaxation.

As they continued their journey, the vibrant energy of Calabar's streets echoed in their hearts. The captivating aroma of street markets, the delectable tastes of traditional dishes, and the lively conversations with locals painted a vivid tapestry of their experiences.

With every step, Mark felt a deeper connection to Calabar's rich cultural heritage. The bustling markets, the tantalizing flavors, and the captivating stories woven into the city's fabric had left an indelible mark on his soul. Just as he had uncovered the beauty of Calabar, he knew that Nigeria's diverse wonders still held much more to be discovered.

❖

Their journey through Calabar resembled a carefully crafted mosaic, woven with threads of culture, history, and delectable cuisine. They delighted in savoring the region's traditional dishes, relishing Afang soup's rich flavors and experiencing the unique taste of Ukwa, a breadfruit delicacy. These culinary delights deepened their appreciation for Calabar's gastronomic treasures.

With hearts warmed and stomachs content, they bid farewell to the enchanting city of Calabar. The memories forged and connections made during their expedition held profound importance. As their travels continued, they carried Calabar's vivacious spirit within them—a constant reminder of Nigeria's diverse cultural splendor and the significance of shared encounters.

Turning towards Mark, a grin played across his lips, eyes alight with anticipation. "Mark, our next adventure awaits in the heart of Nigeria, Abuja, the Nation's Capital. Brace yourself for an extraordinary journey through the core of our country's politics and culture."

Mark's face lit up with eagerness, a radiant smile spreading across his features. "Abuja, the Nation's Capital!" he exclaimed, excitement evident in his voice. "I've heard tales of its grandeur and historical significance. I'm eager to immerse myself in its past, embrace its vibrant traditions, and bear witness to the pulsating center of Nigeria's political landscape. Arinze, this promises to be an unparalleled adventure!"

As they continued conversing, the prospect of exploring Abuja's intricate mosaic of history and culture ignited a fire of enthusiasm within them, propelling their journey forward with a renewed zeal.

TWENTY-SIX

The plane touched down smoothly at Abuja's domestic airport; an undercurrent of excitement palpable in the air. Arinze and Mark disembarked with a gleam of anticipation in their eyes. The city's vibrant atmosphere embraced them, infusing their spirits with a keen sense of adventure.

Unbeknownst to him, his eagerness for this journey was subtly intertwined with a calculated decision. Rather than embarking on the long drive from Calabar to Abuja, Arinze had chosen a more efficient route. He had parked his car at the hotel in Calabar and arranged for his driver to collect it and return it to Lagos. With logistical matters settled, he and his friend took to the skies, journeying to Abuja for further exploration.

As they stepped onto the tarmac, his enthusiasm was contagious. "Mark, let's make the most of our time in Abuja. There's so much to see and experience here."

He nodded; his excitement mirrored in his eyes. "Absolutely. Let's dive into the heart of the city's culture."

He looked around at the busy crowd to find his friend Tochukwu. He suddenly broke out in a big smile when he saw his tall figure moving through the crowd of people with ease. His regal appearance and intricately embroidered agbada showed how deeply he was connected to Nigerian culture.

"My dear brother! Welcome to Abuja!" Tochukwu shouted, and his voice was full of happiness and warmth. As the two friends embraced and laughed, their friendship was rekindled.

He looked at him and put out his hand to greet him. "Hello, Mark! It's great to meet you at last. You are now in Nigeria's capital city, Abuja. Get ready for something that will stay with you forever."

He thanked him for the handshake with all his heart. "Thank you. I've heard great things about Abuja, and I can't wait to find out what it has to offer."

The conversation flowed easily as they walked towards his s sleek black sedan. The three them got into the car and talked as if no time had passed.

His friend, Arinze, was so excited to talk about how much he loved Abuja that he couldn't hold it in. "Mark, get ready to be amazed. Abuja is a city in Nigeria that is unlike any other. It has beautiful buildings, a lot of green space, and a rich mix of cultural traditions. You're in for something good!"

He leaned back and looked out the window at the beautiful scenery. A beautiful urban landscape was made by the wide, well-kept roads lined with lush trees and carefully trimmed gardens. His eyes were drawn to the buildings they passed because they were a mix of modern and traditional styles.

"You were right, Arinze," he said with real amazement. "Abuja is simply breathtaking. I'm really impressed by how well planned and thought out everything is. This city is very proud of its infrastructure and how it looks.

He beamed with pride and couldn't wait to show him more about Abuja's great things. "That's just the start. Wait until you see the beautiful parks, visit the cultural sites, and taste the different flavours of Abuja's food. This city has a lot going for it."

As the car moved through the city streets, the friends kept up their lively conversation and talked more about Abuja's many wonderful things. Their hearts were full of excitement for the exciting adventures that were waiting for them in the beautiful capital of Nigeria.

He gave a satisfied nod, a smile spreading across his face. "Indeed, Mark. Abuja, the administrative capital of Nigeria, is a symbol of the hopes and dreams of our whole country. With everyone's help, we've made a city that makes us all feel proud."

Tochukwu, who was driving the car through the streets with skill, felt compelled to say something. "Let me add, that Abuja is more than just pretty on the outside. This city is truly unique, not only because of the people who live here but also because of the richness of our traditions.

He listened to what they said and felt a deep sense of gratitude for the chance to see the nations capital from the different points of view of his friends. His ideas about Africa were shattered when he saw how beautiful and grand the city was. He was amazed that Abuja and the other Nigerian cities he had been to were better than some of the places he had been to in his home country.

He couldn't help but say how amazed he was as they kept going. "Guys, what you've said is so true. Abuja is a great example of how far Nigeria has come and how beautiful it is. It has really been better than I thought it would be."

He looked at him and smiled warmly. "We're glad to be able to share this with you, my friend. Nigeria has a lot to offer, and we're excited to give you a taste of our interesting and diverse country."

Tochukwu spoke up, and his voice was full of pride. Get ready for a trip to Abuja that you will never forget. From its beautiful buildings to its rich cultural history, this city is sure to leave an indelible mark on your heart.

As the car smoothly drove through the streets, the friends had lively conversations about the unique things that made Abuja so appealing. He was impressed by how rich and deep Nigerian culture was, and he was excited to see what adventures he would have in the country's capital.

❖

He drove his car with ease through the rich streets of Asokoro, a neighbourhood known for being exclusive and wealthy. He was amazed by how big and beautiful his estate was when they got there.

He opened the door and waved proudly at his friends to come in. "Gentlemen, welcome to my humble home. Please feel free to settle in."

He walked into the foyer of the palace, and his eyes lit up with admiration. "This place is beautiful, Tochukwu! You have really made a place of comfort and style."

He smiled and thanked Arinze for his kind words. "Thank you. It's a labour of love and a place where I find comfort and happiness. I'm excited to show it to you both."

As they sat down on the soft couch in the living room, lively conversation and true friendship filled the air. He couldn't help but feel welcome and at home in this beautiful place.

He put his back against the wall and smiled. "I have to say, that your success is inspiring. It shows how hard you've worked and how good your taste is."

He laughed in a humble way. "Thank you. But success doesn't mean much if you don't have close friends like you two."

He looked around to see all the wealth around him. "I have to say, this is not at all what I was expecting. Abuja is full of surprises, from its beautiful buildings to the warm welcome of its people.

He nodded in agreement. "Indeed, Mark. Abuja is a city that goes against common ideas. It's a melting pot of culture and sophistication, where old and new things blend together well.

Arinze spoke up, and his eyes lit up with joy. "And Mark, we've barely scratched the surface. There is so much more to see and do in this amazing city."

His interest was piqued, and his voice showed how eager he was. "I can't wait to learn everything I can about Abuja's rich history. We have a lot to learn about the city, from its historical sites to its lively cultural festivals.

Tochukwu leaned forward and smiled mischievously. "Well, gentlemen, get ready for an adventure like no other. We're in for a lot of surprises in Abuja, and I can't wait to show you what this amazing city has to offer.

Tochukwu assumed the role of a knowledgeable tour guide, steering the car through Abuja's bustling streets while highlighting the city's remarkable landmarks. Mark, his eyes wide with curiosity, absorbed Tochukwu's words like a sponge, eager to soak in every bit of information.

Arinze, his excitement barely contained, turned to Mark with a grin. "Get ready, Mark! Zuma Rock is about to take your breath away. It's this majestic monolith that stands tall just north of Abuja. The stories behind it are as fascinating as its sheer beauty. Some say there are ancient secrets hidden within its massive form. No wonder it's proudly featured on the hundred-naira bill!"

He leaned forward; his gaze fixed on the majestic rock formation in the distance. "Arinze, that is truly incredible! It's a sight unlike anything I've ever seen. It feels as though Zuma Rock carries the weight of history itself, with stories waiting to be discovered."

Tochukwu interjected with a smile. "And let me share with you, my friend, that we are currently passing through the Three Arms Zone. It's where Nigeria's legislative, judicial, and executive branches reside, at the heart of our political system."

He marveled at the imposing buildings, symbols of democratic governance. The House of Assembly, where laws were debated and passed, represented the power of collective decision-making. The Judiciary building exuded a sense of fairness and justice, while the Presidential Villa emanated authority and responsibility.

Intrigued by Aso Rock, the renowned seat of power, he inquired further. His expression turned somber as he replied, "Unfortunately, Aso Rock is not accessible to visitors without special invitations. Given its significance, strict security measures are in place to protect its integrity."

He nodded, understanding the importance of security. "I see. It's fascinating to observe the different approaches countries take to safeguard their vital institutions. It highlights the diversity in governance worldwide."

Arinze, eager to share more, chimed in, "Let me introduce you to the National Church of Nigeria, also known as the National Christian Centre. It's a magnificent place of worship for our Christian community."

Tochukwu added, "And don't forget the Abuja National Mosque, a marvel of architecture and an important spiritual center for Muslims. The doors are open to the public, except during group prayer times."

He marveled at the city's religious landmarks, representing the harmonious coexistence of different faith and traditions. The Abuja National Mosque offered tranquility to the Muslim community, while the National Church of Nigeria stood as a testament to the Christian community's devotion. It showcased Abuja's embrace of religious diversity.

In that moment, he couldn't help but feel a sense of gratitude for the opportunity to witness the city's rich history, culture, and faith. The dialogue, laughter, and shared experiences deepened their bond, creating memories that would endure long after their adventure came to an end.

As they got closer to the Cultural Centre and the tall Millennium Tower, He couldn't hold back his excitement. "Mark, picture yourself standing on top of the tallest building in Nigeria and looking out at the breathtaking view that awaits you! The Millennium Tower shows how far our country has come and how high it wants to go. It is a symbol of our determination to reach new heights.

Mark's excitement bubbled within him, fueled by the thought of reaching the observation deck atop the Millennium Tower. It was like the beginning of a thrilling adventure, and the anticipation was palpable. The audacious architectural feats of Abuja and the city's steadfast commitment to progress had already won a special place in his heart.

As they continued their exploration, Mark turned to Tochukwu, his eyes alight with curiosity. "Tochukwu, I can't wait to experience the view from the Millennium Tower. It's not just a tower; it's like a symbol of Abuja's determination to reach new heights."

Tochukwu nodded; his voice filled with pride. "You're absolutely right, Mark. And you'll see, the view from up there is something truly spectacular."

Soon, they parked and made their way to the Millennium Tower. As they climbed the steps to the observation deck, Mark's anticipation grew with every step. Finally reaching the top, Mark stepped onto the deck and was met with an awe-inspiring sight – the sprawling beauty of Abuja spread out below him.

Arinze couldn't help but grin at Mark's reaction. "Well, what do you think?"

Mark's eyes were wide, his voice tinged with wonder. "This is breathtaking! The city seems to stretch endlessly, a tapestry of lights and life. It's like seeing Abuja in a whole new light."

Tochukwu chuckled. "It has that effect on everyone. The city reveals a different kind of magic from up here."

They spent moments gazing out over the city, taking in the vibrant streets, the mix of modern and traditional architecture, and the pulsating energy that defined Abuja. Mark couldn't help but reflect on his journey across Nigeria and how it had shattered his preconceived notions.

"I never imagined Nigeria like this," Mark admitted, his voice quiet. "The beauty, the diversity, it's all so remarkable. And being up here, it's like I've stepped into a world of endless possibilities."

Arinze clapped Mark on the back. "That's the spirit! Nigeria has a way of surprising even the most seasoned travelers."

Tochukwu grinned. "And this is just the beginning. There's so much more to explore."

As they descended from the observation deck, Mark's heart felt light, his spirit invigorated by the view that had opened his eyes to Abuja's grandeur.

As the car drove through the busy streets, the trio kept up their lively conversations. They told stories, laughed, and learned new things. The words and sounds of Abuja's lively sights and sounds were woven into the natural flow of the conversation. Each historical site they went to helped them grow as people by giving them a deeper understanding and making them question their own ideas and biases.

Their trip to Abuja was more than just a trip to see the sights; it was a life-changing experience. It showed how strong a country is and how much of its potential hasn't been used yet. The nation's capital turned out to be a living example of how beauty can grow in unexpected places and how good people can be anywhere.

His heart filled with gratitude as the car kept going through Abuja. During their travels, they talked, laughed, and made friends, all of which became treasured moments that made memories that would last a lifetime. He realised at that very moment that a place's true personality isn't just made up of its physical features, but also of the stories and connections that are woven into it.

TWENTY-SEVEN

The next night, the trio were excited to go to the famous Cubana Lounge, which is known all over Abuja for its lively atmosphere and never-ending entertainment. This place was like a club, a restaurant, and a hotel all in one. It gave its guests a lot of different things to do. As soon as they walked in, they were thrown into a world full of energy and excitement.

The Cubana Lounge was a feast for the eyes on the inside. The big dance floor invited guests to give in to the pulsing rhythms, and they did so eagerly, giving in to the irresistible pull of the music. Warm and bright lights filled the room, making it feel magical. Every part of the room gave off an air of sophistication and elegance, from the soft seats to the sleek bar.

Absorbing the lively ambiance, Mark's eyes widened with each passing moment, brimming with excitement. "Guys, can you believe how amazing this place is?" he exclaimed, turning to his friends Arinze and Tochukwu, who were equally captivated by the scene.

Arinze nodded, a grin spreading across his face. "I heard the DJ here is something else. Let's see if the hype is real."

Tochukwu chimed in; his voice full of anticipation. "And those beats – they're like a magnet pulling everyone in."

As the DJ skillfully melded an eclectic range of music styles, the crowd remained entranced, every beat a new adventure. Amidst the pulsating rhythms, Arinze leaned toward Mark. "Man, this DJ knows how to keep us moving. This night's just getting started."

Conversations and laughter wove a vibrant tapestry in the air, seamlessly intertwining with the melodic sounds. Mark glanced at Tochukwu. "It's not just the music, it's the energy here. Feels like we're part of something incredible."

Tochukwu nodded in agreement; his gaze fixed on the lively scene. "And check out the food scents from that restaurant area – my stomach's already protesting."

A symphony of delicious aromas wafted from the restaurant, tempting everyone to indulge in mouthwatering dishes. Mark, now comfortably seated, couldn't contain his excitement. "I can't wait to experience everything this place has to offer. It's like a whole new world."

Arinze patted him on the back. "Get ready for an escapade, my friend. Tonight's going to be epic."

Tochukwu raised his glass in agreement. "To an unforgettable night!"

With a shared toast, they settled into their seats, ready to embrace the life-changing journey ahead. The friendly staff, attentive to their every need, enhanced the experience, ensuring their time at Cubana Lounge would leave an indelible mark.

Amidst the pulsating beats, all-encompassing scents, and the company of friends, they reveled in the magic of the moment, poised to dive headfirst into an extraordinary adventure that would forever linger in their memories.

Arinze leaned in and spoke louder than the music. "Mark, get ready to have the best time of your life! The Cubana Lounge is known for its lively atmosphere, great music, and excellent service. Get ready to dance like crazy and make memories that will last a lifetime!"

He nodded, and his eyes were full of excitement. He took in the contagious energy all around him and enjoyed the good vibes that were in the air. The rhythm moved through his body, giving him a strong urge to let go and be fully present in the moment. Strangers were easily able to connect with each other because they were all going through the same thing.

As the night enveloped the city of Abuja, they found themselves entranced by the pulsating energy of the lively nightlife. The club's vibrant atmosphere filled with rhythmic beats and laughter drew them into a state of pure euphoria.

Amidst the dancing crowd, His gaze was captivated by the beauty of the Nigerian girls in their club-like dresses. They exuded confidence and grace as they moved to the music, their radiant smiles lighting up the space. The colorful lights reflected in their eyes, making them even more alluring.

Arinze, with a wide grin, exclaimed, "This is the place to be tonight!"

"Tochukwu, can you believe the energy here?" He asked, excitement in his voice.

He nodded; his eyes gleaming with delight. "It's amazing! Let's dance with these lovely ladies!"

Approaching a group of girls, they introduced themselves with charm and charisma. Conversations flowed effortlessly as they shared laughter and dance moves.

"You guys are fantastic dancers!" one of the girls complimented them.

"We can't compete with your dancing skills," Arinze replied playfully.

Mark, always respectful, engaged in light banter, making sure to keep things friendly. "You ladies have got some serious moves!"

Tochukwu, eager to learn more about the captivating girl he had his eye on, asked her name. "I'm Tochukwu, and you are?"

"I'm Amara," she replied with a warm smile.

As they danced and talked, he felt a genuine connection with her. He admired her vivacious personality and couldn't help but be drawn to her beauty.

"You have a captivating smile," He complimented her, his eyes locked onto hers.

"Thank you," she blushed, feeling flattered by his attention.

As the night wore on, the trio of friends shared their thoughts on relationships. Mark spoke earnestly, "For me, it's important to be a one-woman man. Love should always come first."

Arinze nodded in agreement, "Absolutely, bro. My wife means everything to me."

Tochukwu chimed in, "I have a serious girlfriend, and I'm planning to marry her soon."

Although he felt a connection with her, he remained committed to his relationship. "Amara, I've had a great time talking and dancing with you tonight. Can I have your number to stay in touch as friends?"

She smiled, appreciating his honesty and integrity. "Sure, I'd love that."

He realised in the midst of the excitement that moments like this crossed boundaries and brought people together. It showed how music, laughter, and shared experiences can bring people together and make memories that will last a lifetime.

Their night at Cubana Lounge was a symphony of laughter, dancing, and making new friends. It was a special part of their trip through Nigeria that they would always remember.

He was in awe and deeply moved by how kind and friendly the Nigerian people were. He was shocked by how many people were kind to him, and he ended up talking to people about things that had nothing to do with the event. It was a night of coming together and partying, where everyone forgot their differences and focused on the joy, they all felt.

"Can you believe how friendly people are?" Mark said something, and his eyes lit up with thanks. "I've never met people who were so kind and friendly for real. It's really something."

With a smile on his face, Arinze nodded. "Mark, that's the great thing about Nigeria. Even if you've just met them, our people have a way of making you feel like family. It's all about coming together and having a good time."

He joined the conversation, and his voice was full of joy. "I've talked to people from different walks of life, and it's amazing how quickly we got along. It's like we're all one big happy family, brought together by the happiness of this moment."

As the night slowly came to an end, He went into the next day with a deep sense of gratitude. The Cubana Lounge was a great example of Abuja's lively spirit and its people's ability to make places where people can have fun. He knew that the talks, laughs, and friendships that happened inside those walls would always be important to him. He loved every moment because he knew how important they were to his journey.

"This is the magic of Abuja's nightlife," said Tochukwu with a warm smile. It brings people together, breaks down walls, and makes memories that will last a lifetime. These moments will always remind you of the happiness and togetherness we felt tonight."

He left Cubana Lounge feeling full of energy and with a new appreciation for how appealing Abuja's nightlife is. The night had been freeing and showed what magic can happen when people from different backgrounds get together for a party. The city's lively spirit was ingrained in his mind and served as a constant reminder of how lively Abuja's soul was.

He couldn't help but think about how powerful shared experiences are and how amazing connections were made in that amazing place. It was a great example of how people can work together and how joy can cross boundaries. During that night of partying, Abuja showed him who it really was, leaving a mark on his heart that will never go away.

As they left the city, he took with him the memories of that amazing night, knowing that they would always be a source of inspiration and a reminder of the amazing spirit that lived in Abuja.

He smiled and looked at Mark. "Remember, my friend, you will always have the spirit of Abuja with you. It's a reminder that joy and unity can be found anywhere if we're willing to look for them.

He nodded, and his voice was full of thanks. "I'll never forget this experience or the amazing people I've met through it. Nigeria has left an indelible mark on my soul. It reminds me of the power of celebration and the beauty of human connection.

The trio had left Cubana Lounge with their hearts full of memories and newfound appreciation. They took the spirit of Abuja with them as they went on to their next adventure.

❖

TWENTY-EIGHT

As Mark's journey through Nigeria drew to a close, he bid farewell to Arinze and his family with a mixture of gratitude and anticipation. The time had come for him to return to Toronto, but his heart was brimming with cherished memories, newfound friendships, and invaluable life lessons that he would carry forward.

"I can't thank you enough for everything, Arinze," he said with sincere gratitude. "This trip has made a big difference in my life. I've learned a lot and done things I never thought I'd be able to do."

He gave Mark a warm smile and put a hand on his shoulder. "I was glad to do it, my friend. I'm glad you came to see me and that we got to share these moments together. Remember that Nigeria will always be your home."

He got on the plane to go back to Toronto, but all he could think about was his time in Nigeria. He would never forget the time he spent in Arinze's village during the lively New Yam Festival. It was a party to honour tradition, the community, and how everyone is connected.

He told the person sitting next to him inside the plane, "I never thought I would see such a beautiful festival." "The New Yam Festival taught me how important it is to keep things simple and how connected people really are. It was a lesson in humility."

The other passenger got closer because he or she was interested. "Tell me more. What did you learn while you were there?"

His eyes lit up with excitement as he started to talk about the important lessons he had learned. "The people of

Nigeria taught me how important it is to have real relationships. I saw how important it is to be humble and how beautiful it is to find happiness in small things. It's not about the things we own or the things we do. It's about the depth of our relationships and the effect we have on other people."

As he kept talking about his life and what he had learned, he realised how important it was to share what he had learned.

He said, with conviction in his voice, "I really want to tell people what I've learned." "We live in a world where superficial connections often take the place of real ones. But in Nigeria, I saw how real connections can change our lives in big ways. It's something that needs to be brought up and cared for."

The other passenger agreed and nodded in affirmation. "You've hit the nail on the head. It's easy to get caught up in our own egos and lose sight of the real significance of connecting with others. Your time in Nigeria has truly given you a renewed understanding of what truly matters in life."

Upon arriving back in Toronto, Mark's thoughts were awash with contemplation and a fresh sense of purpose. The journey had realigned his priorities, shifting his focus from mere career advancement to cherishing the significance of family and close relationships. Stepping off the plane at Pearson International Airport, he couldn't shake the feeling that this marked the dawn of a new chapter.

Navigating the customs and immigration process, Mark's mind wandered as he observed the bustling travelers, the frenetic environment, and the familiar Canadian weather greeting him. The overcast sky hinted at impending rain.

Collecting his belongings, Mark's gaze landed on Amanveer, his dependable office driver. The genial Indian man known as Aman for short stood by the car, waving with a welcoming smile from the exit section of the arrivals area. They had coordinated their meeting earlier during a phone conversation.

"Welcome back, sir," he greeted warmly as he approached. "How was your trip sir?"

He returned the smile, appreciating Aman's presence. "It was transformative. Nigeria left an indelible impression on me."

As he walked towards Aman, he also noticed his office assistant, Maria, waiting nearby. she, too, smiled and greeted him. "Welcome back, Mark. We're excited to have you back."

He nodded with gratitude, a sense of familiarity and comfort settling in. "Thank you, Maria. It's good to be back."

Once they were all together at the car, Aman opened the door and gestured for them to get in. As they settled in, he turned to her. "Maria, how have things been at the office while I was away?"

She leaned forward, her tone laced with enthusiasm. "It's been busy, Mark. I've been sending you updates via email as usual, but there's also a significant new development I wanted to discuss in person."

He raised an eyebrow, intrigued. "Oh? What's the new development?"

As Aman started the engine and they navigated through the rain-washed streets, she briefed him on the latest office developments, including some reshuffling in teams and the growing interest in the proposal he had been working on before his trip.

"That's intriguing," Mark mused, absorbing the information. "It seems like my absence hasn't slowed things down."

Maria chuckled. "Not at all. In fact, it's been quite the opposite. Your return will surely bring an added momentum to the team."

The rain continued to gently tap on the car's roof, creating an intimate atmosphere as they drove. Mark looked out of the window, his mind a whirlwind of thoughts about the journey from the airport to his destination – a journey marked by conversations, updates, and the promise of exciting opportunities. As they arrived at his destination, Mark stepped out of the car, ready to embrace the new phase awaiting him, both in his career and in his renewed appreciation for the intricacies of life.

TWENTY-NINE

He told a close friend over coffee, "When I was in Nigeria, I saw how strong family ties are." "My friend and his kind wife, the warmth of their home, and the friends I made all over the country reminded me how important family is." I want to get back in touch with people I've lost and fix things that are broken."

His friend listened carefully and offered help. "Mark, it's never too late to catch up with old friends. Your journey has shown you how important it is to keep in touch with those people. I will always be there for you."

He came back to Toronto with a clearer idea of what he wanted to do with his life and a deeper understanding of how rich human experiences are. The lessons he learned in Nigeria had left an indelible mark on his soul and led him to live a life focused on deeper connections, humility, and personal growth.

He was excited about his new way of thinking and wanted to keep broadening his horizons and making connections with important people. Nigeria had opened his heart and mind and shown him how beautiful every human connection is and how rich it is to be open to new things.

His trip to Nigeria had left a mark on his heart that would never go away. With each passing day, he took on more of the spirit of the country. When he thought back on his time there, he couldn't help but be amazed at how the media spreads false ideas that hide what Nigeria is really like. In his mind, him and his friend Rachel had a conversation that summed up their ideas and thoughts.

Seated across from her, he savored the warmth of their coffee as they delved into a meaningful conversation. Rain pattered lightly against the café window, creating a cozy ambiance that complemented their exchange.

"You know, Rachel," he began, his eyes lighting up, "Nigeria really shifted my perspective. It's incredible how media often portrays it as a dangerous place."

She leaned in, intrigued by his words. "I agree, Mark. The negative portrayal often overshadows the true essence of a place."

He nodded; his expression determined. "Exactly. Nigeria's filled with resilient, compassionate people who radiate life."

Her gaze held a spark of agreement. "People often jump to conclusions based on what they hear, overlooking the nuances."

His enthusiasm grew. "Nigeria has remarkable potential. Imagine if it embraced good governance, accountability, and unity. And its cultural history is a treasure trove."

She leaned forward, captivated. "Their cultural diversity is truly intriguing. It's vital for their identity."

His voice animated, he continued, "Their ability to thrive despite adversity is awe-inspiring. They're masters at making the most of their resources."

A smile played on his lips, reflecting his optimism. "You know, I'm already planning to return someday. I want to explore its varied landscapes, immerse myself in its rich culture, and contribute to its growth."

Her eyes lit up with genuine interest. "That's wonderful, Mark. Your dedication can make a difference. Nigeria deserves a chance to showcase its potential."

A shift in his demeanor signaled a change of topic. "Oh, and guess what? This summer, Arinze and his family are coming to Toronto. They want to experience a Canadian summer once more."

Her face lit up. "That's fantastic news! It's heartwarming how cross-cultural friendships can flourish."

His excitement bubbled. "I'm eager to reciprocate their hospitality, show them around, and have an amazing time together."

As their dialogue ebbed and flowed, the café's cozy environment mirrored their heartfelt conversation. The rain continued its gentle melody outside, creating a backdrop for their connection.

Her smile was radiant. "Friendships that transcend borders are a testament to shared humanity."

His determination shone through. "Exactly. These connections motivate me to strive for my goals. I'm determined to showcase Nigeria's true potential."

Her eyes glinted with understanding. "Your journey is inspiring, Mark. The world needs more people who see beyond stereotypes."

Their conversation, interwoven with pauses and animated gestures, mirrored the rain-kissed window that separated them from the world outside. As they shared thoughts, dreams, and aspirations, their bond deepened, solidifying their resolve to embrace opportunities and foster cross-cultural connections.

THIRTY

Longing for success had always driven Mark, but a recent epiphany had ignited a newfound desire within him – the longing to extend a helping hand to others. His heart now yearned to make a positive impact beyond personal accomplishments.

Devoting his free hours to a local food bank, he immersed himself in volunteer work at the soup kitchen. These selfless endeavors, where he could aid those in need, filled him with a profound sense of purpose and contentment. The act of giving became his source of joy.

Amid the clatter of the kitchen, his eyes fell upon a familiar face – Mike, an old friend who had hit a rough patch. The lines of hardship were etched on Mike's face, an unfortunate casualty of losing his job.

"Hey, Mark," Mike's voice broke through the kitchen's din, "It's been a long time since we've seen each other."

His response carried a blend of concern and kindness, "Hey, Mike." His gaze held a mix of worry and compassion. "What went wrong? What have you been doing?"

His sigh carried the weight of recent struggles. "I lost my job and had to move. It's been tough, my friend."

His concern deepened, and a resolve began to form. He couldn't stand idle while his friend was struggling. He leaned in, his determination shining through. "Listen, Mike, I've been thinking. I want to initiate a program to assist people facing situations like yours. I'll leverage my business connections to help them secure jobs and provide support when they need it most."

Hope ignited in his eyes. "Wow, that's incredible. Right now, I could really use your help."

As he recognized the significance of his mission, the weight of the moment settled upon him. Still in the midst of the soup kitchen, his mind buzzed with ideas. After the last meal was served, he and Mike delved into the specifics of the program.

He exited the busy kitchen at the local food bank, but a sense of purpose had enveloped him. He knew the path ahead wouldn't be easy, but he was prepared to put in the effort. He was resolute in his commitment to aid those in need, fortified by the support of his friends and family.

He followed through on his promise, scheduling regular meetings with Mike and others facing challenges. During these discussions, they dove into their aspirations and necessities. He also tapped into his network, passionately sharing the program's objectives and rallying for assistance.

He was taken aback and deeply grateful by the outpouring of support. People stepped up to help – finding employment opportunities, offering advice, and even contributing financially. Overwhelmed by the genuine care he encountered; Mark felt tears welling up. He understood that this was just the beginning of an extraordinary journey.

Devoting substantial time, he meticulously crafted a detailed plan of action for the program. He enlisted volunteers like Rachel and his friend Alex's wife, Emily – individuals equally dedicated to the cause. United by a shared purpose, they tirelessly organized fundraisers, engaged potential employers, and provided guidance to program participants. His happiness soared as he realized the tangible difference he was making in people's lives.

Under the sunlit sky of a serene Sunday afternoon, he embarked on a journey to reconnect with his children at Sarah's house. Amidst the city's bustling streets, he found solace in life's unhurried moments. The vibrant urban tapestry unfolded before him as he meandered through the streets.

Amidst his contemplations, his attention was caught by a familiar sight. In the adjacent lane, Mike was confidently steering a sleek black sports car. A wide smile lit up his face, a silent celebration of Mike's transformed life through his program. Brimming with excitement, he rolled down his window and hailed, "Hey, Mike! Long time!"

Mike's surprised expression quickly melted into an earnest smile. "Mark! Check out this car! Your program turned my life around."

Both cars found their way to the roadside, aligning in a spontaneous symphony. Their shared destination, a busy street corner, became an impromptu reunion spot. As they emerged from their vehicles, their warm embrace bridged the gap between their individual journeys.

During their animated exchange, Mike expressed profound gratitude for Mark's instrumental role in reshaping his life. Face-to-face interaction had been Mike's intention, yet Mark" his voice held a sincere undertone, "your transformation and the positive changes you've experienced fill me with immense joy. I ask of you one thing."

He leaned in, intrigued and attentive. "What is it?"

His eyes ignited with resolve. "Pay it forward, Mike. Utilize your newfound success and the lessons you've garnered to guide others treading similar paths. Let your journey be a beacon for those still seeking their way."

His nod conveyed his profound understanding. Mark's words had kindled a sense of duty within him, compelling him to reciprocate. With a determined grin, he pledged to share his transformative experience, continuing the cycle of positive change.

Their conversation echoed with laughter, reflections on their distinct journeys, and visions of a brighter future. He bid Mark farewell, their embrace cementing a promise of ongoing friendship and shared aspirations. Gratitude-filled meetings and a steadfast bond spurred their shared commitment to uplift and empower.

Returning to their vehicles, his gaze lingered on Mike's striking sports car, a symbol of achievements earned through hard work. Side by side, the two vehicles embodied distinct journeys woven together by resilience and mutual support. Amidst life's challenges, their friendship illuminated the potential for positive transformation through unwavering determination and the spirit of giving back.

As Mark drove away from the street corner, a renewed sense of purpose infused his thoughts. The conversation lingered in his mind, casting ripples of contemplation. He understood that this chance encounter had ignited an even fiercer determination within him – the determination to effect change, one person at a time. Amid the ebb and flow of the city, he found himself fixated on the promises woven on that very corner, a promise to create ripples of transformation.

Lost in his musings, the intrusive ring of his phone startled him. His fingers deftly navigated the steering wheel of his powerful GL 350 Mercedes-Benz, skillfully pressing the answer button. "Hey, Mike! Still feeling inspired?" he chimed in with an air of curiosity.

On the other end of the line, Mike's laughter resonated, carrying a note of familiarity. "Absolutely, Mark! The conversation we had lingers. I've never felt more resolved to grow as an individual and impact others positively."

His heart warmed at his words. "I share your sentiment, my friend. It's awe-inspiring how a single conversation can stir such profound change. Let's continue down this path together, empowering those around us."

Amidst the rhythmic hum of the engine and the city's soundscape, their dialogue continued, weaving dreams and aspirations. The phone line crackled with an infectious enthusiasm, a testament to the power of compassion and its ability to create waves of transformation.

As he maneuvered through the urban currents, his gaze flitted across the faces of anonymous passersby. A thought ignited within him, prompting him to pull over. In the cocoon of his Mercedes, he drafted a message to Mike, proposing a collaborative venture that could amplify their impact.

"Hey, Mike! What if we orchestrated a community event to disseminate positivity and drive tangible change? Imagine gathering to share our journeys, inspiring others to embark on the same path."

His response reverberated through the quiet of the car, a swift affirmation of their shared purpose. "Mark, count me in for that idea! Together, let's empower others to undergo the same transformative journey."

Together, we can show them the power of kindness and the way it can make things better for everyone."

They were enthusiastic to put their plan into action. They kept talking on the phone, talking about logistics and coming up with ideas for how to make their community event impactful and memorable.

The next week, they met in person to make sure everything was set. As they sat in a cosy café, they talked about the dreams and goals they both had.

He savored a sip of his coffee, his eyes igniting with a contagious excitement. "Imagine the joy people will experience when they realize they possess the power to shape the world. This event has the potential to infuse hope and ignite a ripple of positive actions."

He nodded in sync with his fervor, his expression mirroring shared enthusiasm. "Absolutely, Mark. We've witnessed firsthand the transformative might of compassion. Now, it's our turn to equip others with the tools they need to foster kindness and catalyze change within their own communities."

Around them, the energy in the downtown Toronto lounge owned by none other than music superstar Drake was palpable. It buzzed with their fervent discussions, the air charged with determination and shared visions. Their camaraderie solidified, a union of intent driving them toward the shared objective of crafting a better tomorrow.

As plans unfurled, logistics were ironed out, and visions for the event crystallized, the lounge reverberated with their collective energy. Every conversation carried the resonance of their shared purpose, echoing their unity in creating a brighter future.

Leaving the lounge that day, they departed with a renewed sense of purpose. Gratitude swelled within them – gratitude for their friendship and the opportunity to embark on this transformative journey side by side. Their hearts brimmed with anticipation for the path ahead, confident in their capacity to effect change and uplift lives.

While driving home, Mark's keen observation caught the tapestry of small acts of kindness woven into the fabric of the city's bustling streets. A smile curved on his lips as he comprehended the immense potential held within each seemingly insignificant gesture. He recognized that even the smallest deeds had the power to touch lives and set forth a domino effect of positivity.

THIRTY-ONE

Anticipation and gratitude filled Mark's heart as he prepared for the long-awaited reunion with his sister. The prospect of Sarah bringing their kids to the same event intensified his excitement and stirred a well of hope within him. This upcoming gathering held significance beyond measure – a pivotal juncture to mend their fractured relationship and bridge the gaps that had long kept them apart.

Amid the flurry of preparations, memories from the past resurfaced, drifting through his mind like fragments of a puzzle. They transported him to a critical conversation with his sister Jennifer, a conversation that had reshaped their dynamic. Well before his journey to Nigeria and the pivotal advice-seeking talk with Arinze, he revisited that turning point when they had reconnected. The gravity of their exchange remained imprinted, compelling him to unravel its implications.

His thoughts journeyed back to a quiet café corner where he had shared a coffee with his sister. The air held a palpable sense of anticipation as the silence stretched between them. His voice, a blend of remorse and determination, eventually pierced through. "Jenny, that crucial conversation we had before my trip to Nigeria – it lingers in my thoughts. It altered my perspective completely."

She regarded him, a mix of curiosity and caution in her gaze. "What do you mean, Mark? That conversation was a turning point for both of us."

With a solemn nod, he met her gaze earnestly. "Your courage in addressing your pain made me realize how my pride had corroded our bond. My vulnerability during that time made me see the change I needed."

A softer glint graced her eyes; her voice held a blend of vulnerability and optimism. "I recall that moment vividly. It took courage on my part to confront you, but I'm glad I did. It was a crucial step towards healing."

Emotion quivered in his voice; his sincerity evident. "Jenny, I deeply apologize. I own my mistakes and their impact. I'm committed to change, to setting things right."

Tears glistened as she absorbed his heartfelt words. She saw the truth in his eyes, the authenticity of his transformation. "Mark, I appreciate your apology and your efforts to change. It's a journey, but your actions reflect your sincerity. I'm cautiously hopeful about the road ahead."

Their conversations became a tapestry of shared memories, woven across time. Laughter punctuated their dialogue as they revisited cherished moments, allowing the warmth of their relationship to gently mend old wounds. He observed the evolution of her pain into a tentative hope, witnessing the once-barren realm of sibling reconnection begin to bloom.

As time unfurled, their talks delved deeper, bridging the chasm that had festered for years. His eagerness to transform and her willingness to extend a chance fostered an environment of trust and mutual comprehension. With each passing day, their relationship gained resilience – a testament to their capacity to forgive, evolve, and love unconditionally.

Amidst contemplation, the sharp honk of a car broke through the reverie, jolting him to the present moment. Through the window, he glimpsed Sarah's vehicle gracefully pulling into the driveway. A rush of emotion coursed through him as his children stepped out, laughter dancing in the air. The scene was a mosaic of rekindled connections, a canvas painted with the hues of shared love and the promise of a harmonious future. They ran into their father's arms and gave him hugs and shouts of joy. It was a moment of pure happiness.

Soon after, Jenny's car pulled up next to them in a stylish way. His heart soared when he saw Jenny's kids get out of the car and smile. They ran towards their uncle with great excitement. When they hugged him, it was clear that their love had stood the test of time.

As they all got together, laughter and warmth filled the air as the family hugged each other for the first time in a long time. Mark couldn't help but feel overjoyed and grateful for this chance to fix things between them.

Sarah looked at him with a warm smile and said, "I'm so glad we were all able to get together like this. It shows how much we've grown and changed over the years. Our children deserve a family that loves and sticks together."

He agreed, and tears of happiness filled his eyes. "Yes, you're right. All of us are starting over now. I'm glad we have the chance to fix our broken relationships and give our kids a better future.

Jenny moved closer, her voice a blend of emotions. "Mark, I can see the change in you, and I appreciate the effort you've made. Rebuilding trust takes time, but I'm willing to give it a shot. Let's focus on our love for each other and create new memories together."

He extended his arms, embracing her warmly. "Thank you, Jenny. Your willingness to give me another chance means a lot. Let's move forward with open hearts and strengthen our sibling bond."

After their heartfelt moment, Jenny turned to Sarah, sharing a genuine hug and exchanging pleasantries.

Mark interjected with a smile, "Nigeria truly worked its wonders on me. It's been transformative."

When the kids saw this show of love and peace, they were filled with happiness. Esther., Mark's youngest child, spoke up. Her voice was pure and full of hope. "Daddy, I'm so glad that we're all here. Can we start over and live happily as a family?"

Mark's eyes filled with tears as he gave Esther a tight hug. "Yes, honey, of course. This is where we start over. We will enjoy every moment and work together to make the future full of love, understanding, and happiness."

The family laughed, told stories, and made new memories as the day went on. As they focused on the present and loved the chance to fix what was broken, the pain of the past slowly went away.

He stood at the beginning of a new part of their lives, thankful for the journey that brought them here. The reunion showed not only that he was back in touch with his sister, but also how important it is to forgive and how strong family bonds are.

At that moment, he realised that their meeting was more than just a visit. It was a rekindling of love, a healing of broken hearts, and a celebration of how second chances can change lives.

The weekend was like a symphony of laughter, sharing stories, and getting to know each other better. Mark's house had a new feeling of togetherness. It was a safe place where memories were made and hearts were healed. The kids loved having their cousins around, and their laughter could be heard all through the house.

He was filled with gratitude as he watched the interactions. Seeing his children, nieces, and nephews get along and make connections that would last their whole lives gave him a deep sense of happiness. It was a reminder that even though life can be hard, love and forgiveness have the power to heal even the deepest wounds.

As the weekend came to an end, there were a lot of different feelings in the air. Sadness and gratitude mixed together, because the time they had spent together had reignited a flame that had gone out. Sincere promises were made to keep building on the new connections that had been made.

He gave his kids a tight hug and told them goodbye until their next get-together. As they left, he could still hear their laughter in his ears. Jenny stayed a little longer, her eyes shining with tears of happiness and relief.

She said, "Thank you, Mark," in a whisper that was full of emotion. "What this weekend meant to all of us can't be put into words."

Mark hugged his sister and held her close. The bond between them was stronger than ever. "Thank you for giving me this chance to make up for what was lost," he said with sincerity. "I am very thankful, and I promise with all my heart to treasure and care for our relationship."

As she drove away, he felt a sense of peace come over him. The eco of sounds of laughter and love could still be heard, which showed how strong the human spirit is and how important it is to forgive. He knew that they would have to keep working at getting better, but that as time went on, their relationship would get stronger.

He stood in the quiet of the evening, listening to the sounds of happy times. His heart was full of hope. The way to peace had been made clear, and he promised to follow it with unwavering commitment. For in the arms of his family, he had learned what love, forgiveness, and the ties that bind us all really meant.

THIRTY-TWO

His steps took him through the old, busy park. This was a place where he and Sarah used to love and have fun. It just so happened that the park was close to where they had lived together when they were first married. He felt a wave of nostalgia when he saw an old man struggling to carry his groceries.

He felt sorry for the man and went up to him to offer help. "Excuse me, sir. "Can I help you carry those bags?"

The old man looked up, and his eyes showed a mix of surprise and thanks. "Oh, boy, that would be so helpful. The weight of these bags seems to have gone up over time."

He smiled, and the old man's praise warmed his heart. "I'm glad to do it. By the way, my name is Mark. "What are you called?"

The old man smiled back, and when he did, his eyes got kind. "I'm Robert. Mark, it's nice to meet you."

Strolling side by side, their dialogue ebbed and flowed effortlessly, touching upon shared interests. His attention was drawn to Robert's eyes, where he glimpsed reflections of his own history. It was as though destiny had guided him to this very spot – the entrance of the apartment complex where he and Sarah had once woven their dreams together.

His voice had a bittersweet tone as he looked around at the familiar places. "Robert, it's amazing how memories can come flooding back all at once. This place reminds me of stories from my whole life."

Robert nodded. He knew how heavy nostalgia could be. "Ah, the power of places to make us feel things and remember things we had forgotten. It can be beautiful and painful at the same time."

He went on, but his voice was a little sad. "Sarah and I began our journey together in this building. We put love and hope into everything. People laughed and cried in these rooms."

Robert listened carefully, and his eyes showed that he had seen and done a lot in his life. "These precious, happy and sad moments make us who we are today. Life is a tapestry made of both happy and sad things."

Mark's voice got softer as he talked about their neighbours and how they had built a sense of community. "The hallways echoed with the sounds of people walking, so we could talk to our neighbours. They were more than just names on a list; they became friends who shared smiles, stories, and a sense of belonging.

Robert nodded, and thoughts of his own town came back to him. "A tight-knit group of people is a rare gem. It gives life to the things we do every day and turns strangers into friends who walk with us on this journey.

Mark's voice in the lift was full of reverence as they went up the floors. "Each floor has a memory that changed our lives, like a wedding anniversary, a birthday, or the birth of our first child. The walls were there when we fell in love."

Robert's eyes lit up with warmth as he agreed with what was being said. "A home becomes a sign of love and a place to keep memories. It's where a family's heart beats, where traditions are made, and where secrets are safe."

Still, Mark felt heavy as he walked back through the familiar hallways. "These walls also absorbed our fights, the echoes of angry words that now echo in the places where love once grew. It reminds me of the cracks that got bigger without anyone noticing and caused distance and pain.

His footsteps led them to the living room, which used to be a safe place for them. He stopped for a moment, his hand hovering over the doorknob as memories pressed down on him. He felt a lot of different things, like love, loss, and the complicated nature of relationships.

Robert put a gentle hand on his shoulder and said, "I know what you're going through." "Sometimes, our hearts are heavy with both happy and sad memories. It's a sign of how strong our feelings are and how complicated love is."

He met his gaze, gratitude filling his eyes. "Right on, Robert. We broke up because of pride and misunderstandings, but today I choose to put the past behind me. Now, my goal is to help other people, be humble, and bring back what was lost."

Robert's smile showed that he was wise. "A noble endeavour, Mark. Don't forget that the biggest changes start with small acts of kindness and a willingness to fix what's broken."

He nodded, and he suddenly felt like he had a reason to fight for all that his inordinate ego had cost him. "Thank you, Robert, for what you said. They've touched my heart and it will help me stay on the right path. I'll use the lessons I've learned here as I try to make peace, promote understanding, and show the humility that makes real connections possible.

He said goodbye to the old man with a handshake, knowing that their chance meeting had made a big effect in him. He was now more determined to continue to ask for forgiveness, heal old wounds, and live a life based on humility, forgiveness, and love.

As he walked away, he felt grateful for the past and determined to continue to make the future a better place. The lessons he learned now would continue to stay with him and guide him towards peace, understanding, and the power of humble connection.

His footsteps echoed through the park, carrying a bittersweet blend of sorrow and hope. As he walked, he found himself immersed in his thoughts, contemplating the path ahead, the mending of fractured relationships, and the cultivation of profound humility that would allow him to cherish and nurture the bonds that truly mattered. The lessons learned had ignited a flame within him, urging him to embark on a journey of transformation.

Suddenly, raindrops began their gentle dance upon the window pane, matching the rhythm of his contemplation. Just then, his phone rang, and the name "Dave" illuminated the screen. His voice softened as he answered, knowing too well the weight of his friend's battle with depression. Dave's struggles had deeply touched him, instilling a profound sense of empathy.

With unwavering patience, Mark listened intently as Dave poured out his heart, sharing the hardships he faced. His voice trembled with vulnerability, seeking solace and understanding from a friend who had weathered his own storms.

"Mark, it's been so hard... Everything feels overwhelming," Dave confessed, his voice laced with sadness.

Mark's empathy flowed through his words as he responded, "I understand, Dave. I've treaded through those dark waters too, and I know how exhausting it can be. But remember, you're not alone in this journey. I'm here for you, and together, we can navigate these turbulent seas and find the strength to sail onward."

His voice cracked with relief, gratitude seeping through his words. "Thank you, Mark. Your presence, your understanding... it means the world to me. Your own journey gives me hope that I can find my way back to the light."

Mark's heart swelled with a renewed sense of purpose, knowing that his experiences had the power to offer comfort and guidance to others. "You're never alone, my friend. We all stumble and falter at times, but together, we can rise above the darkness and discover a brighter path."

As the conversation came to a close, Mark turned his focus inward, reflecting on the transformation he had undergone. He marveled at how humility had replaced pride, and empathy had blossomed from within. Each step taken had led him closer to the person he aspired to be.

Peering out the window, his eyes were drawn to a magnificent rainbow gracing the sky. Its vibrant arc painted hope across the horizon, a reminder of the resilience of the human spirit. The sight filled him with reassurance and reinforced his commitment to a life guided by humility and compassion.

"I'm ready," he whispered to himself, inspired by the radiant spectrum overhead. "Ready to spread empathy, kindness, and understanding wherever my journey takes me."

With renewed determination, he embarked on the next chapter of his life, vowing to uplift others, offer solace in times of need, and be a beacon of hope in a world that yearned for compassion. The symphony of transformation played on, its melody composed of humility, empathy, and the unwavering belief that small acts of kindness could create a ripple effect of change.

THIRTY-THREE

He found peace in his new office, which was quiet and peaceful even though it was late at night. The room gave off an air of sophistication and power, which was a great match for his new position as Chief Operating Officer. It was a reminder of what an amazing journey he had been on.

He was sitting at his desk when his mind wandered as he thought about how far he had come.

"Maria," he said as he looked over at his trusted assistant, who was sitting at the desk next to him. "Can you believe we've come so far? The road we've gone down together?"

She looked up from what she was doing and smiled softly.

"Every day, Mark," she said with admiration in her voice. "It's amazing to see how much you've changed over time. You have really grown into a great leader."

He reclined in his chair and gazed out at the city skyline, illuminated like a captivating panorama of dreams.

"The city below," he said, with a tone of gratitude in his voice, "reminds me of all the chances I've had." This office and these walls represent the chances I've had.

She agreed, knowing that what he said was important.

"You've earned every bit of it," she said with affection. "Your journey of thinking about yourself and growing as a person has been nothing short of amazing. This office and your job as Chief Operating Officer are proof of that."

His eyes moved to his beautiful mahogany desk, which was a sign of power and responsibility.

"This desk," he said next, his voice full of respect, "is more than just a piece of furniture. It shows the weight I carry and the mix of tradition and new ideas I have to deal with when making important decisions."

Her eyes followed his and took in the desk's beauty.

She said with admiration in her voice, "You have a unique ability to bring together the past and the future, tradition and progress. It makes you stand out as a truly great leader."

He turned his attention to the soft leather chair that was waiting for him. It would give him comfort as he faced the challenges ahead.

"This chair," he thought with a soft but determined voice, "will be my safe place." A place where I can get my thoughts together and get ready for the opportunities and problems that lie ahead."

She nodded to show that she understood and that she knew how important this space was.

"A leader," she said, "needs a safe place to think, a place to make decisions that are well thought out. Mark, this chair will do you good."

His eyes went to the carefully chosen art on the walls. Each piece was full of creativity and inspiration.

"The art," he said with excitement in his voice, "it speaks to me. It makes me think of new ideas, and I hope it does the same for other people. I want this office to be a place where people can be creative and feel free to try new things.

She looked at everything on the walls and liked how much thought had gone into each choice.

"You've made a place where people can work together and be creative," she said with admiration in her voice. It shows that you have a clear vision and want to create an excellent environment."

Hiss eyes then went to the cosy corner, which was made to be a place where people could talk and share ideas informally

"And that cosy corner," he said with a hint of excitement in his voice, "is where connections are made and great ideas are born. I want people to feel comfortable and know that their opinions matter."

She smiled, knowing how important it was to have a place where people could talk informally.

"It's the little things," she said, "that make this office more than just a place to work. You've made a place where people can really thrive and where collaboration thrives."

He leaned back in his chair, happy with how things were going.

"When I'm in this office, bathed in the soft light of the moon," he said, "I feel a purpose that goes beyond these walls. I'm ready to take on my new role as COO, not only because of what I've done, but also because of what I've learned.

She looked at him and gave him her full support.

"Together, Mark," she said, "you'll motivate, inspire, and build a workplace culture that values collaboration, empathy, and a never-ending quest for excellence. Your life experience has given you special skills for this, and I'm sure you'll leave an indelible mark."

With unwavering resolve, he gave a firm nod, solidifying his stance.

He thought back to the conversation that changed the course of his career and said, "And it all started with that one important conversation."

His mind went back to that life-changing moment, and the words were burned into his memory.

He whispered, "I can still hear his voice," with a touch of longing in his voice. "They liked my progress and how hard I worked to improve myself. "Maria, it meant the world to me."

Her smile got bigger, and she looked proud.

"It was an honour that you deserved, Mark," she said. "Your unwavering commitment and humility have helped you get where you are now. Now you're getting what you've worked for."

He turned his attention back to the city below. He felt like he had a new sense of purpose.

"From this office," he said with conviction, "I have a duty to lead with humility and kindness. I'll use my newfound power and influence to help the people around me live better lives. With you by my side, Maria, we'll be able to handle the problems that lie ahead."

They felt the weight of their shared goal as they sat in the quiet of the office. They were ready to start a new chapter, having learned a lot and formed a strong bond.

THIRTY-FOUR

He found himself alone in his office as Maria, his assistant, stepped out into the outer office. With a moment of solitude, his mind drifted back to the conversation he had with Kenneth, the Chief Executive Officer. His voice echoed in his ears, resonating with hope and trust as he delivered life-changing news.

"The board has recognized your tremendous growth, Mark," Kenneth had shared, his tone brimming with anticipation. "They have decided not only to unfreeze your promotion but also to appoint you as the Chief Operating Officer."

His heart skipped a beat as the weight of the news settled in. This moment was a culmination of his hard work, a testament to the transformation he had undergone and the impact he had made within the company. Yet, instead of pride rushing through his veins, a deep sense of gratitude washed over him, accompanied by a renewed commitment to serve with humility.

Leaning forward, the CEO locked eyes with him, his gaze filled with sincerity. "Mark, your journey has been nothing short of inspiring," he commended. "You have demonstrated the immense power of humility, not only in transforming individuals but also in shaping entire teams. I have full confidence that if you continue on this path, you will be ready to lead this company as CEO when the time comes."

The weight of his words overwhelmed him. A profound sense of responsibility gripped him as he considered the trust and faith others had placed in him. This promotion meant more than a mere rise in status or compensation;

it was an opportunity to make a difference, to uplift others, and to lead with humility.

In that moment, he had recognized that his journey towards humility was far from over. The promotion marked not the end, but a new beginning—an invitation to continue growing, learning, and contributing to the success of the company and the well-being of its employees.

Expressing his heartfelt gratitude with a humble smile, He thanked the him for the remarkable opportunity. Silently, he made a solemn promise to live up to the trust others had bestowed upon him, to lead with compassion, and to foster a corporate culture rooted in humility and kindness.

As he departed from his office, he carried with him a profound sense of gratitude and purpose. The promotion not only symbolized his professional growth but also stood as a testament to the progress he had made in overcoming his ego and embracing humility.

Recalling the celebratory party held in his honor, he reminisced about the joyful atmosphere that filled the venue. Vibrant decorations in his favorite colors set the stage for a jubilant occasion.

Entering the party, he was greeted with cheers and applause. Colleagues, who had once whispered behind his back, now approached him with warm embraces and messages of congratulations. The room buzzed with happy conversations, laughter, and an energy befitting a joyous celebration.

One by one, coworkers shared stories of how his transformation had inspired them and positively impacted their work lives. They expressed their appreciation for his kindness, understanding, and willingness to listen. He was deeply touched by their heartfelt words, realizing the profound influence he had on their lives.

As the night unfolded, he found himself engrossed in profound discussions with coworkers hailing from various departments. These conversations acted as a bridge, repairing strained relationships and nurturing a sense of unity among the diverse team. The gathering transformed into a symbol of shared purpose, as disagreements took a back seat to the pursuit of collective goals.

Whistles and comments of agreement filled the air as his words resonated with his colleagues.

Amid the friendship and genuine connections, a realization struck him—he wasn't on a solitary journey towards humility, but rather a catalyst for positive change within the company. Filled with a renewed sense of purpose, he embraced this responsibility. His commitment to growth, empathy, and humble leadership was unwavering.

Colleagues cheered and clapped, knowing they were part of this transformative journey.

As the evening's events drew near, he stood before his coworkers, his eyes brimming with gratitude. With a sense of spontaneity, he delivered an unscripted, heartfelt speech:

"Tonight, I stand before you, overwhelmed with gratitude and humility. This gathering, this party, is a celebration not just of my personal journey, but a testament to the remarkable power of change and the incredible support each one of you has provided.

A chorus of applause greeted his opening words, demonstrating the unity in the room.

As I reflect on where I was merely a few years ago, I realize I was blinded by pride and self-centeredness. I could never have fathomed standing here today, surrounded by colleagues who have transformed into friends and friends who are now family. It's a truly humbling experience.

A colleague shouted, "You've come a long way, Mark!" The sentiment was met with cheers of agreement.

I want to extend my heartfelt thanks to each of you. Your belief in me, your challenges, and the opportunities you've given me to evolve and change have shaped me profoundly. Every interaction, every conversation, and every shared moment has left an indelible mark on me.

People nodded and clapped, acknowledging the impact of their collective support.

I still remember when hushed whispers accompanied my presence. Back then, I was oblivious to the negative impact of my actions on our work environment and relationships. But all of you, my colleagues, have taught me the importance of kindness and understanding. You didn't give up on me; instead, you extended a helping hand when I needed it most. You demonstrated the significance of humility, active listening, and treating others with kindness and respect.

A coworker shouted, "You've become a role model for us!" The room erupted in agreement, punctuated by supportive cheers.

I am truly grateful for the conversations we've shared, both professional and personal. Your stories—your struggles, your triumphs—have taught me the importance of caring deeply for one another and the immense power we hold to influence each other's lives.

A voice chimed in, "We're all in this together!" The phrase was met with resounding agreement.

As we gather to revel in tonight's festivities, let's not forget the journey that brought us here. A journey defined by growth, empathy, and the incredible strength of forgiveness. Together, we've nurtured a workspace where collaboration thrives, trust prevails, and respect binds us.

Applause and enthusiastic shouts of "Yes!" and "Absolutely!" filled the room.

I want each of you to understand that without your unwavering support, I wouldn't have undergone this transformation. You gave me a second chance, and I am committed to making the most of it.

Colleagues clapped with a fervor, expressing their collective belief in his potential.

Let's continue ensuring that every individual feels valued, that their ideas are cherished and shared, and that we uplift each other to reach unparalleled heights. Together, we possess the power to achieve greatness and create a positive impact on the world around us.

Shouts of encouragement and support echoed through the room, creating an atmosphere of shared determination.

Thank you, from the depths of my heart, for aiding me on this journey. Thank you for your unwavering faith in me. And thank you for affording me the opportunity to not only grow as a professional but also as a human being.

Colleagues clinked their glasses together, accompanied by cheers and applause.

Here's to the potential of change, the resilience of our collective spirit, and the multitude of possibilities that lie ahead."

Thunderous ovation, punctuated by the echoing applause and jubilant shouts, filled the room as Mark's speech concluded.

The resonance of his speech in the room was palpable. The party stood as a pivotal juncture—a celebration of personal growth and the newfound respect Mark had earned. The experience emboldened him further, solidifying his commitment to a life defined by humility and kindness, with the knowledge that he could wield transformative influence on those around him.

The room buzzed with excitement and heartfelt conversations, as colleagues shared their thoughts on the powerful speech.

Carrying the memories of that remarkable evening with him, he found himself reinvigorated. The event served as a constant reminder of the progress he had made and the person he had evolved into. He cherished the love and support he had received, vowing to continue impacting the lives of others positively.

Colleagues approached him with warm smiles and congratulatory pats on the back, reinforcing the strength of their camaraderie.

The party marked a substantial stride in his journey, igniting a passion within him to approach the future with humility, gratitude, and an insatiable hunger for personal growth. As he retraced his steps to that special night, a profound sense of contentment enveloped him, affirming that his metamorphosis wasn't just an individual transformation, but a force for change in the lives of everyone he encountered.

Laughter, joyful anecdotes, and shared memories filled the room, as the atmosphere remained charged with positive energy.

Emerging from his reverie, him grounded himself in the present moment. He took a deep, deliberate breath, savoring the tranquil ambiance of his new office. The tasteful furnishings, the soft glow of ambient lighting, and the sprawling cityscape outside all stood as poignant emblems of the transformative path he had undertaken and the mantle of responsibility he now shouldered.

As his gaze swept across the room, it lingered on the framed photographs resting upon the shelves. Among them were snapshots of his family, friends, and coworkers—each image a portal to cherished memories. Nostalgia welled up within him as he beheld these pictures, each one a visual narrative that recounted moments of significance and the connections he had forged.

His eyes settled on a particular photograph, one that held a complex mixture of emotions. It was a picture of his family, captured during a time when he was still married to Sarah. The image depicted a seemingly happy unit, their smiles belying the underlying tensions that ultimately led to their separation. Although both he and Sarah had moved on and were now divorced, he had chosen to keep this photograph—a keepsake of what pride had cost him. It was a poignant reminder of the fracture that pride had inflicted upon his family, a solemn memento of what had been lost.

A twinge of melancholy accompanied his thoughts, as he contemplated the roads not taken and the paths that had diverged from that point in time.

Yet, beyond the weight of regret, the photograph held a glimmer of hope. It was a testament to his willingness to mend, to heal, and to hold onto the possibility of reconciliation. The image of the family they once were spoke of his enduring optimism, a silent prayer that the universe might one day conspire to knit their family back together.

A mixture of emotions washed over him, a blend of remorse and anticipation, a poignant acknowledgment of the past and a yearning for a different future.

As he stood before the photograph, the echoes of his speech from the memorable party resounded in his mind. The image took on new layers of meaning, representing not just a personal journey, but the interconnected journeys of all those who stood alongside him—family, friends, and coworkers alike. Each person in that photograph had played a role in shaping him, in guiding him towards a path of humility and growth.

A deep sense of connection settled upon him, a recognition of the interwoven threads of life that bound them all.

He took a deep breath, drawing strength from the memories that the photograph invoked. The image encapsulated a chapter of his life, a chapter he would continue to carry, not just as a reminder of what was, but as a beacon of hope for what might be. With renewed determination, he turned away from the photograph, ready to embrace the present moment and the possibilities it held.

His heart felt lighter, infused with a newfound resolve, a commitment to embrace both the memories and the future with open arms.

The framed pictures on the shelves remained as silent witnesses, each one a portal to a different facet of his journey. As he moved forward, he carried their stories within him, a testament to the connections that had shaped him, the lessons he had learned, and the hope that persisted despite the passage of time.

The room held a quiet ambiance, a reflection of the thoughts and emotions that had been stirred within him. And as he stepped away from the photographs, he did so with a heart brimming with a unique blend of sentiments—reflective, hopeful, and ever-evolving.

THIRTY-FIVE

The tranquility of the office was interrupted by a gentle knock on the door, pulling him back into the present. As he turned towards the sound, he was greeted by the familiar face of his trusted coworker and friend, Chiamaka.

"Hey, Mark," Chiamaka greeted with a warm smile. "Can I come in?"

A wave of delight washed over his face. "Absolutely, Chiamaka," he replied warmly. "Please, come in."

Stepping into the office, she effortlessly radiated a sense of ease and unity, her eyes taking in the elegant ambiance of the space.

"Whoa, Mark," Chiamaka exclaimed with admiration, her eyes sparkling. "This office is truly remarkable. You've worked so hard for it all."

He nodded, a blend of gratitude and humility gracing his expression. "Thank you, Chiamaka. The journey to reach this point has been incredible, and I couldn't have accomplished it without the support of an exceptional co-worker like you."

Her smile widened; her eyes filled with pride. "Mark, you've truly come a long way. From the challenges you've faced to the personal growth you've undergone; your journey has been nothing short of inspiring."

Moved by her unwavering support, he approached her with appreciation. "Chiamaka, you've been there for me every step of the way. Your hard work, insights, and constant support have been invaluable. I feel incredibly fortunate to have you as my co-worker and friend."

A moment of silence enveloped them, allowing the weight of their impact on each other's lives to settle in. The office, adorned with tasteful decorations and emanating a professional atmosphere, symbolized their shared commitment to growth and collaboration.

His eyes gleamed with excitement as he spoke, his voice brimming with purpose. "Chiamaka, I've been reflecting on my journey thus far and the valuable lessons I've learned. I believe it's time to give back and share my knowledge and experiences with others who may be navigating similar paths."

Her curiosity sparked; her eagerness evident. "What do you have in mind, Mark?"

Leaning back against his desk, he gazed out the window, absorbing the expansive view. "I envision workshops, mentorship programs, and other initiatives aimed at fostering humility and kindness in the workplace. By sharing my stories, I hope to inspire others to embark on their own transformative journeys."

Her face lit up with a bright smile, mirroring his enthusiasm. "Mark, that's a fantastic idea. You have the potential to make a profound impact, not just within our organization but in the lives of many individuals as well."

He nodded, determination emanating from his every fiber. "Precisely. My experiences have underscored the importance of cultivating environments where empathy, understanding, and teamwork can flourish. By pursuing these endeavors, I aim to effect lasting change and inspire others to embrace humility and kindness."

Standing together in the office, the room pulsated with the promise of their shared vision. They delved deeper into his ideas, forging plans, discussing the individuals and groups who could benefit from their assistance.

As the night went on, their shared goal filled them with more and more excitement. They knew there were problems ahead, but they didn't let that change their minds. They were all working towards the same goal and stood at the beginning of a new part of their journey, ready to take on the possibilities that lay ahead.

He was right on the edge of making a big change in his life at that pivotal moment. The elegant decorations in his office and the energy in their shared vision were clear signs that they were ready. His desire to spread humility and kindness burned brightly, and he hoped that this would start a chain reaction of good changes that would reach far beyond their workplace.

They were excited about the vast horizons that lay ahead of them. Their minds were full of ideas and their hearts beat with purpose. They were ready to bring their vision to life, to change people's lives, help them grow, and leave an indelible mark on the world. They set out on this shared mission with a strong sense of purpose and the belief that their combined efforts would make a big difference.

"Mark, I think your trip to Nigeria was a big part of how you changed as a person," she said, with admiration in her eyes. "Experiencing different cultures and seeing the problems people face can change a person's view of the world in a big way. I can't believe how much you've changed."

He nodded, and a feeling of thanks filled his body. "Thank you. My time in Nigeria did show me how important empathy is and how important it is for people to work together. It has made me more determined to make a positive difference, not just in our organisation but in the world as a whole.

Her face shone with joy. "Indeed, your journey has given me and everyone else around us a lot to think about. Our team wants to make positive changes because of how hard you work to be humble and kind. I'm sure that if we all work together, we can make a workplace that encourages kindness, growth, and inclusion.

As they talked about the possibilities of their shared mission, they talked about important issues like social justice, sustainability, and getting involved in the community. She talked about recent things that had happened in Nigeria, focusing on examples of resilience and grassroots movements that had caught her attention. He listened carefully, enthralled by the stories and inspired by the activists' and survivors' spirits.

He said with admiration in his voice, "I am amazed by how strong and determined people are when things don't go their way." "Their stories show how much power we have as individuals to make a difference. It shows how important it is to develop a sense of empathy and a sense of collective responsibility."

She nodded, and her eyes showed that, she was sure. "Absolutely. We can only make changes that last if we all work together. We can help make the world a fairer and more caring place by encouraging dialogue, understanding, and openness, both within our organisation and beyond.

As the day went on, they talked more and more about how to promote diversity and inclusion, how to deal with environmental problems, and how to help local communities. Their shared vision grew because they both wanted to make a positive difference.

Their hopes and dreams filled the office, which was now full of purpose and potential. It had become a place where ideas took off, where people got the power to do things on their own, and where a group mission to make a change in the world came to life.

During that life-changing moment, they realised how much power they had as forces for good. Their shared experiences, which were fueled by empathy and a desire for justice, had given them a common goal. They were ready to challenge the status quo, give a voice to those who weren't heard, and make a place where compassion and acceptance thrived.

They were fired up and ready to take on the challenges that were ahead of them. Their conversations led to new ideas and connections that helped them work together to solve important problems. They did what they did because they all believed that their actions, no matter how small, had the power to change the lives of people and communities.

The sun fell and it as was office closing hours, they left the office with a renewed sense of purpose and a strong desire to make their shared vision a real thing. They knew the road ahead would be hard, but they were encouraged by the fact that their efforts as a group could make lasting changes and leave an indelible mark on the world.

His reputation started to change over time. Outside his work place people who used to think he was haughty and only cared about himself started to see him as a kind, humble person who was always willing to help. People liked him because he was kind and worked hard to make the world a better place.

THIRTY-SIX

She was completely immersed in the peace and quiet of her new home, a haven of calm in the middle of a busy suburban neighbourhood. The tasteful decorations in the room gave off a soft glow, which was enhanced by the soft light coming in through the windows. It was a safe place that she and her loving husband, Chris, had worked hard to make. His constant support had become the foundation of her new life.

She sank into the soft comfort of her favourite armchair and let her mind wander through her heart's complicated pathways. Mark was her ex-husband and the father of their two beloved children. As she thought about her happy life now, memories of a sad moment with Mark came back to her mind. Even though she was with Chris, she couldn't deny that she still liked Mark. The weight of this realisation mixed with the happiness she felt in her current relationship.

During a recent visit to his house, where she had dropped off the kids for the weekend so she and her husband could have some alone time, an unexpected and intriguing event occurred. It all began when Sarah walked into Mark's house to find a table set for lunch with an array of her favorite dishes. The aroma of the food filled the air, and she couldn't help but be impressed by Mark's thoughtful gesture. The kids were already eagerly sitting at the table, and Mark insisted, along with their pleas, that she join them for the sumptuous meal. Unable to resist, Sarah accepted the invitation, her curiosity piqued by the spread before her.

As they enjoyed the delicious meal together, the atmosphere was surprisingly comfortable. They laughed and shared stories, and for a while, the complications of their past seemed to fade into the background. After the plates were empty and satisfied smiles adorned their faces, the task of clearing the table awaited them.

Working side by side, they gathered the dishes and utensils. Sarah took some of the plates to the kitchen, where the sound of running water filled the space. As she stood at the sink, washing the plates, she felt a presence behind her. Without looking, she knew it was him. Their hands brushed against each other as they both reached for the same plate, and an electrifying connection surged between them.

Their hands touched, and the air seemed to crackle with tension, the moment hanging in the balance as if time itself had paused.

Her heart raced, its rhythm echoing in her ears, and she felt the same energy pulsating from Mark. Uncertainly, their fingers intertwined, the sensation foreign yet familiar. They found themselves caught in each other's gaze, their eyes locking in a way that seemed to communicate beyond words. The cadence of their heartbeats seemed to synchronize, the rhythm of two souls that had shared so much.

In a split second that felt both eternal and fleeting, their lips met, a touch as delicate as a whisper. The kiss conveyed years of history; emotions that had never truly been resolved. Her mind spun with a mixture of longing and confusion, her consciousness a blur of sensations.

But as quickly as the kiss had transpired, she regained her footing. The reality of the situation slammed back into her consciousness, and an instinctual urge to retreat surged within her. She began to step away, her mind a whirlwind of thoughts, her heart in disarray.

Yet, his hand, steady and gentle, caught her sleeve. He drew her back, and while his voice held an undertone of apology, his eyes were resolute. "Sarah, I'm sorry... but I can't deny that I still care about you."

The words hung in the air, a declaration that echoed with a truth they both understood. The complexity of their emotions was laid bare, vulnerable yet undeniable.

Her gaze locked onto his, a mixture of emotions churning within her. She could feel the intensity of his feelings mirrored in her own. The weight of their shared history, the connection that had endured despite time and distance, was palpable.

Her voice trembled slightly as she responded, "Mark, I'm married to Chris, and I love him. But I can't ignore that there's a part of me that still feels for you."

His eyes held a mixture of understanding and vulnerability, a reflection of his own complex emotions. "I get it, Sarah. Our past is a part of us. We've shared too much to simply erase those feelings."

Their hands remained entwined, an unspoken acknowledgment of their entangled past and the powerful connection they shared. The air was charged with a sense of suspended time, a crossroads where the past and present intersected.

His grip on her sleeve tightened gently. "I'm not asking you to change anything, Sarah. Your happiness with Chris and the well-being of our children are paramount."

She nodded, her expression a blend of gratitude and understanding. "Thank you for understanding, Mark. Our history matters, and it's crucial that we navigate this with care."

As they stood there, the kitchen around them seemed to fade into insignificance. The moment encapsulated their journey, the complexities of love and relationships, and the importance of facing those complexities with honesty and empathy.

The room remained hushed, a cocoon of emotions that enveloped them, even as the world outside continued to move forward.

His gaze held a mixture of regret and acceptance, his voice soft yet firm. "We'll find a way through this, Sarah. For the sake of our children and for our own peace of mind."

As the weight of the moment settled in, her grip on his hand slowly loosened. She turned away from the sink, leaving the half-washed plates behind. Tears welled up in her eyes, a tumultuous blend of emotions making her vision blur. With a swift, almost hurried motion, she managed to choke out a quick goodbye to the kids who were engrossed in their games in the living room. Their innocent laughter and playful banter only served to amplify the intensity of her feelings.

Without casting a glance in his direction, who stood framed in the doorway of the kitchen, his gaze locked on her every move, she hastened towards the exit. The path she took through the living room was a blur, the sounds of the games and the children's chatter a distant echo in her ears. Her heart raced as she stepped outside, the cool breeze hitting her face in stark contrast to the turmoil that raged within her.

She hurried to her car, her movements almost automatic, fueled by the overwhelming whirlwind of emotions that consumed her. As the engine roared to life and the familiar hum of the car enveloped her, she found herself gripping the steering wheel, her knuckles turning white.

With a final glance at the house, she had just left behind, the house that held both memories and newly stirred emotions, she took a deep, shuddering breath. Her vision blurred once more, her tears falling freely as she blinked rapidly to clear her sight. The past and the present collided in her mind, and she knew that she needed space, air, and solitude to untangle the mess of emotions that threatened to overwhelm her.

Without another look back, without a word spoken or a gaze exchanged, she put her foot on the pedal and drove away from the house that held a myriad of memories—some cherished, some painful. The road stretched out before her, a path into the unknown, a journey of self-discovery and reconciliation.

The car's engine growled and tires hummed against the asphalt, the sound of her departure a stark punctuation to a chapter that had been momentarily rekindled and then left hanging in the balance.

Mark, still standing in the doorway, watched as the taillights of her car disappeared into the distance. His face was a mirror of mixed emotions—concern, understanding, and a hint of regret. He knew that their encounter had opened a door to a realm of emotions that had been buried beneath the surface, but he also knew that the complexities of their lives couldn't be unraveled in a single moment.

A sigh escaped his lips, a breath he hadn't realized he had been holding. The kitchen, once a place of shared meals and conversations, now felt like a sanctuary of unspoken words and unresolved feelings.

As the door closed behind him, he turned away from the kitchen, his thoughts a whirlwind of introspection. The presence of their intertwined hands still lingered on his skin, a reminder of the profound connection that had momentarily rekindled.

The house settled into a quiet, a stillness that contrasted the tumultuous emotions that had just unfolded within its walls.

He closed his eyes briefly, the memory of their shared past and the weight of the present colliding within him. He knew that they were both on separate journeys, lives that had taken divergent paths. But in that moment, as he stood in the threshold of the kitchen, he couldn't shake the feeling that their paths, though distinct, were somehow still intertwined.

With a heavy heart, he turned away from the kitchen and walked back into the living room, where the echoes of the kids' laughter still lingered in the air. The games continued; the children unaware of the complex emotions that had played out just moments ago.

And as he immersed himself in the joyful chaos of the present, a part of him remained tethered to the bittersweet moment that had unfolded in the kitchen—a moment that had reopened old wounds and stirred dormant feelings, leaving a trail of uncertainty and introspection in its wake.

As her gaze rested upon the photograph of Chris, her heart wavered between the warmth of the memories it held and the lingering pull of her shared history with Mark. The image portrayed Chris's smile—brimming with genuine affection and unwavering love. He had been her constant support during trying times, a pillar of honesty, patience, and enduring devotion. Yet, the specter of her past with Mark continued to cast its shadow, drawing her back into its intricate web.

The experiences they had weathered together, the commonalities they shared, and the resurgence of their connection—all these factors tugged at her heartstrings, evoking a longing for the bygone days and the potential future they could hold.

Amid her contemplation, a deep sigh escaped Sarah's lips. She acknowledged the complex journey that lay ahead, one that required her to confront her history, confront her own feelings, and find a path through the maze of emotions while remaining true to herself. It was a moment to embrace honesty, not just with Chris, but with herself.

Her thoughts crystallized into resolve, and she recognized that it was time to have an open and transparent conversation with Chris. A conversation about the tumultuous feelings that swirled within her, the struggle to reconcile her past with her present, and the internal battles she faced.

With the image of Chris before her, she whispered a silent prayer—an invocation for strength and guidance. It was a way for her to harness her inner fortitude, to prepare herself for the vulnerable discussion ahead. She knew that Chris deserved her honesty, and she was determined to give him just that.

The weight of her decision rested upon her shoulders, a blend of apprehension and determination urging her forward.

As Sarah contemplated her choice, she found solace in relinquishing control and placing her faith in a higher power. She realized that there was a certain comfort in surrendering to the journey, to allowing herself to be guided by forces beyond her understanding. With a quiet sense of resolution, she decided to offer up her prayers—seeking guidance, understanding, and the strength to navigate the path before her.

Amid the tranquility of her home, enveloped by the promises of the present and the echoes of the past, Sarah took a deep breath. Her heart beat in rhythm with a mixture of hope and trepidation, ready to embark on a journey where uncertainty lay ahead. She embraced the unknown, her faith acting as her compass, guiding her toward unexpected twists of love and fate.

Just as her thoughts began to solidify, a gentle tap on her shoulder jolted her back into reality. She turned, her eyes meeting the gaze of Chris, her new husband, who stood before her. The connection between them was a reminder of the present—the love they shared, the life they were building together. In his eyes, she saw a mixture of curiosity and concern, an unspoken question hanging in the air.

As their gazes locked, Sarah's heart fluttered. The weight of her thoughts and the impending conversation pressed upon her, but she drew strength from the love in Chris's eyes. With a mixture of determination and vulnerability, she knew that their journey together would be shaped by the choices she was about to make—the choices that would bridge the gap between her past and present, and lead her towards an uncertain yet hopeful future.

Sarah turned to Chris with a soft but firm voice. Her heart was full of mixed feelings. A soft but firm voice emerged from Sarah's lips as she looked into Chris's eyes. Her heart was a mosaic of mixed feelings, each piece representing a different facet of her complex emotions.

Yet before she could utter her thoughts, Chris's voice, like a soothing breeze, interrupted the moment. "A penny for your thoughts, sweetheart," he said with a gentle smile, his words laden with curiosity and affection.

"Chris, there's something I need to tell you," Sarah began, her voice a mixture of sincerity and apprehension. "I can't hide the truth from you. The feelings I still have for Mark—they're real. The bond we shared, the challenges we faced together, they've resurfaced."

Chris's expression was a blend of concern and understanding. He reached out, gently taking Sarah's hand into his own, a silent gesture that conveyed his willingness to listen and support.

"Sarah, I know your history with Mark is a part of who you are today," Chris replied, his voice gentle but steady. "It's only natural for memories and emotions to resurface, especially when you share children with him."

Sarah nodded, her gratitude evident in her tear-filled eyes. "Chris, you've always been there for me, loving and supporting me through everything," she said, her voice tinged with emotion. "I can't thank you enough for that."

Chris's grip on her hand tightened, his touch a reassurance of his unwavering presence. "Sarah, I chose you too. I love you deeply. You've been my pillar, giving me unwavering love and strength. What we have together is invaluable to me."

His words enveloped her in warmth, a cocoon of security amid the whirlwind of emotions. "Thank you for being so understanding," she said, her voice a whispered confession. "I want to be honest with you, Chris. When I went to drop off the kids at Mark's, something happened. We kissed."

Chris's initial reaction was a mix of surprise and hurt, his features betraying his emotions. However, in a heartbeat, he recollected himself, his expression softening as he looked deeply into Sarah's eyes.

His grip on her hand remained firm, an affirmation of his commitment. "Sarah, I won't pretend that it doesn't hurt to hear that, but I also know that our love is built on trust and understanding. I believe in our future together."

Sarah's heart swelled with a complex blend of emotions—gratitude for Chris's understanding, guilt for the pain her confession caused, and hope for their shared journey. "Chris, your understanding means the world to me," she said, her voice full of sincerity. "I want us to face this challenge together, with open hearts and honest conversations."

Chris's reassuring grip tightened, a silent promise that he was in this with her, every step of the way. "You're not alone in this, Sarah. We'll navigate this journey together, step by step. Our love is strong enough to overcome anything."

Sarah found solace in his words, a renewed sense of hope blossoming within her. "I believe in us," she said, her voice a quiet affirmation. "With your support and our faith, I know we can find the right path forward."

Chris's gaze held hers, a blend of unwavering commitment and understanding. "Let's trust the journey, Sarah. Whatever comes our way, we'll face it together."

In that moment, as their hands remained entwined, they held not just each other's hands, but the promise of a future marked by resilience, honesty, and the unbreakable bond of love.

THIRTY-SEVEN

His legacy continued to swell with the passage of time. His recently published book, a repository of the transformative lessons he had amassed during his life-altering journey, had ascended the ranks to become a best-seller, resonating with people across the globe. A sought-after speaker, he traversed diverse countries, expounding on the significance of humility and kindness. His impact exceeded his wildest projections.

Yet, amidst the accolades and burgeoning fame, an undeniable yearning nestled within his heart. It was a yearning to rewrite his story with his ex-wife, Sarah. The persistent belief that their love remained dormant, awaiting the opportune moment, continued to tug at him.

One day, as he sat basking in the warm sun on his front porch, an unexpected call disrupted his solitude. Alex, an old friend and confidant who had journeyed with him through thick and thin, was on the line. Excitement and admiration-tinged Alex's voice as he extolled the transformation, he saw in him.

"Mark, I've been closely following your journey, and I'm astounded by the person you've become!" Alex exclaimed. "Your change is remarkable, and it's palpable in the impact you have on others."

His kind words swelled Mark's heart with gratitude. He recognized that his metamorphosis wasn't solely self-forged; the guidance and support from people like him had played a pivotal role. The path of humility and self-discovery had been arduous, yet he had persevered due to the unwavering loyalty of friends.

As they conversed, they revisited shared experiences and the wisdom gathered along the way. He couldn't help but share the recent weekend he had spent with Sarah, a moment that had stirred his heart.

"Alex, it was truly magical," he shared earnestly. "When she arrived with the kids, I had prepared her favorite lunch. We all gathered, exchanging laughter and reminiscing—it felt like being reunited with long-lost family."

Alex absorbed his words, fully understanding the significance of the encounter. He sensed the weight of that fleeting moment—an exquisite blend of nostalgia and the promise of renewal.

"And then, Alex," he continued, his tone carrying both excitement and doubt, "as we cleared the table in the kitchen, our hands brushed against each other. It happened while she was washing the plates, and I brought the remaining plate into the kitchen. Our hands brushed against each other—it was as if the old chemistry and our unbreakable bond were rekindled in that simple touch."

A gasp of realization escaped Alex, comprehending the profundity of the occurrence. He knew that he must have been besieged by a whirlwind of emotions—a tapestry woven from history and potential.

Yet, just as quickly as the sparks flared, she regained her composure. Swiftly collecting her belongings, she left him with a kiss imbued with unspoken meaning—a testament to the past and the myriad possibilities that lay ahead.

His heart raced as he revisited that passionate kiss, a convergence of souls in a vulnerable instant. It symbolized a love that transcended words—a silent, resolute force that had withstood the trials of time and the pitfalls of pride.

In that profound moment, his heart metamorphosed into a canvas adorned with the hues of history, the intensity of shared experiences, and the depth of his feelings. The past, present, and future coalesced, whispering the enduring truth that ignited love remains an unwavering flame, persisting through the challenges of life.

Even though she left quickly, leaving him wanting more, he held on to the hope that had come from their meeting. The universe seemed to hint that they might get a second chance, a chance to rediscover how much they loved each other and start over.

As their talk came to an end, Alex gave him some words of support and encouragement. He said that he thought he could handle this tricky situation with integrity and wisdom.

He thought about how hard this journey would be to patch up things with Sarah, he knew that patience and persistence would be his best friends. He never gave up on making his children feel loved, and he treasured every moment they spent together. And when it was time, he would take a leap of faith, hoping that fate would make it possible for them to be together again.

He kept telling his story and inspiring people with his message of humility and the power of real connections. He was more determined than ever. He knew that what he had been through could change people's lives and encourage them to put relationships first in their pursuit of success.

He felt at peace as the sun went down below the horizon and cast a warm glow over the porch. He knew that even if his dreams didn't come true, the love he had found again with his children was a gift that would be with him on his journey. And in that love, no matter what the future held, he found comfort and a glimmer of hope for a better day.

Deep down he knew that true love had a way of finding its way and weaving its threads into the fabric of life. And he accepted the uncertainty with unwavering hope, knowing that fate would lead him to a future where love would win again over past pride.

With a smile on his face as the night fell and the stars began to shine. The world was full of opportunities, and he was ready to take advantage of each one. He knew that love, in all its forms, would always be there for him to be his guiding light.

Both ran into each other at a local charity event on a cool autumn evening as the colourful leaves turned into a dizzying array of colours. They met by chance because they both wanted to make a difference in the world.

When their eyes met, it was as if they both knew something but didn't say it. Even though months had passed, the love they once had was still written in their hearts, a silent sign of how strong their bond was.

They took advantage of a rare quiet moment during the busy event to get away from the noise. In their talk, they went back and forth between talking about the past and talking about what they had learned along the way. Each word said carried the weight of hope and openness, rekindling a fire that had never really gone out.

He felt like he had to act quickly because he felt like time was running out. This was a chance he had been waiting for a long time, and he couldn't waste it. He reached out for her with hands that were shaking and a heart full of feelings. His voice was full of sincerity.

"I've always loved you, Sarah," he said in a voice that was barely above a whisper. "It has stood up to time and the ups and downs of our journey. I know we were meant to be together deep down."

Her eyes filled with tears as her heart struggled with a lot of different feelings. Her love for Mark and her love for Chris, fought each other. She felt the weight of her choices, and she didn't know what the future held.

She said, "I've never stopped loving you, Mark," and her voice shook with raw emotion. "But I've made promises and agreements that I have to keep. I need time to sort out my feelings and get a better view of things."

He knew how hard their situation was because he had grown up and learned the value of patience and respect. Love couldn't be forced; it had to be given space to grow. He gave in to her request for more time with a heavy heart because he knew that their shared journey would be hard to navigate.

They went their separate ways to think and reflect as the weeks turned into months. Even though they wanted to be together, they knew it was important to keep the promises they had made to themselves and to other people.

Then, one day when the cherry blossoms were turning the world pink, he got a letter. It was a letter that showed how weak they were and how much they had in common. It showed how brave they were to face the unknown territory of their feelings.

Her words ran all over the pages, telling Mark how much she loved him and how they had always been close. She was honest about her struggles and the things she had to give up. She was looking for a way to keep the promises she had made to her new husband while still loving Mark.

His eyes filled with tears of both happiness and sadness as he read her truth. Even though the complexity of their situation was hard on him, a new sense of hope grew in his heart. He knew that their love story wasn't over by a long shot.

He felt a twinge of regret during the sweet times he spent with his children. He knew that his pride and the mistakes he had made had caused him to lose her the first time. She was happy with her marriage, so she told Mark to look for a friend and let someone new into his life. Still, he held on to a tiny bit of hope and dared to dream of a magical turn of events that would bring them back together.

He knew in his heart that waiting and hoping might be the only thing he could do. He decided to enjoy the time he had with his kids, help them get along, and let the universe do what it needed to do. His path was clouded with doubt as he tried to figure out what was right and wrong based on what he wanted and what he had learned from his mistakes.

Since that poignant encounter in which they shared an electric kiss, the dynamics between Sarah and Mark had subtly shifted. Gone were the days when she would drop off the kids at his house; instead, a new routine emerged. Mark took the initiative to pick up the kids himself, orchestrating a careful dance that often-involved Chris's presence.

When the moment came for the kids to transition between households, Chris became a constant figure by Sarah's side. Their interactions were punctuated with knowing glances exchanged between Chris and Mark—a silent acknowledgment of the intricacies at play. A few nods here and there, laden with unspoken understanding, further underscored the delicacy of the situation.

The trio's orchestrated routine was a symphony of shared responsibilities, unspoken emotions, and the thread of connection that bound them all. The unspoken conversations, the palpable tensions, and the uncharted territory they navigated bespoke the complexities of their intertwined lives. Through this new pattern, they found themselves dancing on the precipice of unspoken desires and unexplored possibilities, each step a reflection of the intricate balance they sought to maintain.

So, he set out on a journey of patience, ready for whatever twists and turns the future had in store. The sound of his children laughing became a comfort to him and a reminder of the happiness he had found in their company. He was determined to embrace the unknown. He thought that love and fate would eventually come together in ways that were both surprising and miraculous.

THIRTY-EIGHT

At the early hour of 4 am, Mark found himself lying wide awake in bed, his mind a whirlwind of thoughts centered around the upcoming speaking engagement. The invitation he had received to address the delicate interplay between relationships and work had ignited a mix of excitement and challenge within him. As he shifted restlessly, the significance of the topic he had chosen for the seminar, "Maintaining Real Relationships in the Pursuit of Success," weighed heavily on his thoughts.

The invitation, which held the prestigious insignia of the Gottman Institute, had arrived unexpectedly in his email inbox a few weeks ago. The subject line had read, "Exclusive Speaking Engagement: Exploring the Nexus of Relationships and Success." Mark vividly recalled the mix of surprise and elation that had coursed through him as he read the message. The Gottman Institute, renowned for its pioneering research on relationships, was extending an invitation to him – an acknowledgment of his insights and expertise on the very topic that had shaped his career.

As he replayed the memory of receiving the invitation, Mark's thoughts drifted back to his journey as a relationship counselor and motivational speaker. His commitment to understanding the intricacies of maintaining genuine connections in the midst of professional pursuits had led him to pen insightful articles, engage in thought-provoking podcasts, and deliver impactful talks at various forums. His passion had caught the attention of the Gottman Institute through a serendipitous conversation at a recent symposium where his perspectives had resonated deeply with a fellow speaker who happened to be associated with the Institute.

With a sense of humble accomplishment, Mark marveled at the privilege of being chosen as one of the VIP guest speakers for the upcoming event. The Institute's recognition of his work was a testament to his dedication, and he felt a profound responsibility to deliver a talk that would honor the essence of the topic and inspire those in attendance. The opportunity to share a platform with renowned experts in relationships and psychology was both an honor and a challenge that fueled his commitment to providing meaningful insights.

As the hours ticked away and dawn approached, Mark's mind continued to race with ideas, anecdotes, and research findings that he planned to incorporate into his talk. The soft glow of his laptop illuminated the room as he delved deeper into his preparations, driven by a potent blend of anticipation and a genuine desire to contribute to the understanding of relationships and success.

He muttered to himself, "How can I deliver a powerful speech that resonates with the audience? How can I inspire them to prioritize their relationships while striving for success?"

In the days leading up to the event, he had immersed himself in intense preparation. He researched extensively, seeking stories and examples to bring his message to life. With each passing day, his excitement grew, along with his desire to make a meaningful impact on the attendees.

He thought, "I need to connect with the audience on a deep level. I want to share my own experiences, the lessons I've learned, and offer practical advice that they can apply to their own lives."

The day of the highly anticipated event finally arrived, and His heart raced with a potent blend of nervousness and excitement. As he stepped out of the private jet that had brought him to JFK Airport, Maria, his diligent personal office assistant, was right beside him, her eyes reflecting the same mixture of emotions.

"Maria," he said with a half-smile, "can you believe we're here? This moment feels surreal."

She nodded, her voice filled with awe, "It's truly a remarkable journey you've been on, Mark. I'm honored to be a part of it."

As they descended from the aircraft, he couldn't help but marvel at the luxurious interior that had been his home during the flight. The plush leather seats, polished wood accents, and the panoramic views had made it a journey of both physical and emotional comfort.

"Mark," she commented, "this jet is like a world of its own. It's as if success has become your constant companion."

He chuckled, "Success may be the passenger, but it's the people who've believed in me, like you, Maria, who have made this journey truly extraordinary."

The chauffeur, holding open the door to a sleek limousine, greeted them. "Welcome, sir, ma'am. The Majestic Theatre awaits."

Settling into the luxurious limousine, her excitement was palpable. "Mark, can you believe we're heading to the Majestic Theatre? It's legendary!"

He nodded, a smile tugging at his lips. "It's a place where dreams come to life, Maria. And tonight, we're going to add to its history."

As they made their way through the vibrant streets of Manhattan, He couldn't help but overhear her quiet musings. "I've read about this venue, but seeing it in person is something else. The energy here is electric."

He nodded, looking out at the bustling city. "It's like New York itself is welcoming us to share our story."

Upon arriving at the Majestic Theatre, the anticipation in the air was palpable. The sight of reporters and photographers lining the red carpet was both exhilarating and humbling. As they stepped out of the limousine, the flurry of questions from reporters filled the air.

"Mr. Mark, over here! What inspired your journey?"

"Maria, how do you feel being a part of this incredible success?"

He turned to Maria with a grin. "Looks like you're getting your share of the spotlight too, Maria."

She chuckled, "I'll try not to hog it all, Mark."

As they navigated through the crowd, he couldn't help but notice the organizers' efforts to ensure his safety amidst the paparazzi frenzy. It was a whirlwind of flashes and questions, and he appreciated the support.

Inside the Majestic Theatre, her eyes widened as she took in the opulent surroundings. "This place is breathtaking."

"It certainly is," he replied, his voice carrying a mix of pride and gratitude. "And it's going to be the perfect setting for what we're about to share."

As they mingled with attendees and event staff, he couldn't help but overhear snippets of conversations.

"I came here specifically to hear Mark speak. His book changed my perspective."

"Did you see the press frenzy outside? His impact is truly global."

His heart swelled with appreciation for the attendees who had come with such enthusiasm to hear his message. He turned to Maria and whispered, "It's moments like these that remind me why we do what we do."

❖

In a corner of the auditorium, a special VIP section had been reserved for distinguished guests. He sat there alongside Maria, his personal office assistant, who had been an integral part of his journey. They exchanged a few words, a mix of excitement and anticipation evident in their expressions.

As the event progressed, the moment of anticipation drew near. The Master of Ceremonies, dressed in elegant attire, approached the podium. The hushed murmurs in the audience subsided as all eyes turned towards the stage.

❖

It was a sunny morning in the cosy town where Sarah, Chris, and their children lived. She had been scrolling through her email when she stumbled upon a message from her sister, Alana, who lived in Manhattan, New York.

her emails were always filled with warmth, and this one was no different.

"Hey sis!" the email read. "We've been missing you all so much. Why don't you guys come over for a visit? It's been ages!"

Her eyes lit up as she read the email. She turned to Chris, who was sipping his coffee at the kitchen table. "Chris, look at this! My sister is inviting us over for a visit to New York!"

He looked intrigued. "New York, huh? That could be fun. And the kids would love it too."

After a bit of discussion and excitement, they decided to take Alana up on her offer. The idea of a family trip to the bustling city was exhilarating. Little did they know that their journey would lead them to an unexpected encounter.

Fast forward a couple of weeks, and Sarah, Chris, and the kids were on a plane heading to New York. The excitement in the air was palpable, especially for the adults, who were looking forward to exploring the city. They had left the kids back at home, in the capable hands of nannies and alongside Alana's own children.

Upon landing, they were greeted by Alana and Michael. The reunion was joyous, and they quickly caught up on each other's lives. Over dinner that night, Michael revealed an exciting plan.

"Guess what, guys?" Michael said with a sly smile. "There's this amazing event happening in Manhattan soon. It's at the Majestic Theatre, and I managed to get some tickets. I thought it could be a fun outing for us!"

Sarah and Chris exchanged curious glances. "An event at the Majestic Theatre?" Chris mused. "That sounds like a fantastic opportunity."

Sarah nodded in agreement; her interest piqued. "Absolutely. It'll be a great way to enjoy an evening out."

Little did they know that Michael had conveniently omitted one crucial detail – the guest speaker for the event. As they headed to the Majestic Theatre on the event day, their excitement was palpable. They left the kids in the Nanny's care, knowing they were in good hands.

As they entered the theater, the grandeur of the venue left them in awe. The bustling atmosphere, the elegantly dressed attendees, and the anticipation in the air all added to the mystique. Alana and Michael led the way, guiding them to their seats.

Sarah leaned over to Chris and whispered, "I'm so glad we came. This place is stunning!"

He nodded, a smile on his face. "Definitely. It's been a while since we've been to an event like this." Alana leaned over to Sarah and whispered, "Can you believe how grand this event is, sis? I'm so glad you guys could make it."

She nodded, a smile on her lips. "It's truly impressive, Al. And the kids are having a blast at your place with their nannies and your children."

Chris chimed in, a playful glint in his eye. "Yeah, it's a vacation for everyone. Thanks for having us over."

As the event began, the Master of Ceremonies took the stage, introducing the guest speaker with enthusiasm.

As the event progressed, the moment of anticipation drew near. The Master of Ceremonies, dressed in elegant attire, approached the podium. The hushed murmurs in the audience subsided as all eyes turned towards the stage.

"Ladies and gentlemen," the MC began with a charismatic smile, "thank you for joining us tonight for this extraordinary event. We have a special guest among us who has graced the global stage with his insights and wisdom."

The spotlight gradually shifted to Mark in the VIP section, drawing the audience's attention to them. Maria's eyes glinted with pride as she looked at Mark, knowing how far he had come on his transformative journey.

Sarah's heart skipped a beat as she recognized Mark's face. Her eyes widened, and she turned to Chris, a mixture of shock and disbelief in her expression.

"Chris," she whispered urgently, "that's... that's Mark."

"It is my privilege to introduce a man who needs no introduction," the MC continued, his voice resonating throughout the auditorium. "He is not only an acclaimed speaker but also an author whose words have struck a chord across the world. His best-selling book, 'Forgos of the Ego,' has become a global phenomenon, touching hearts and inspiring change."

As the MC spoke, the audience's excitement rippled through the air. People leaned forward in their seats, eager to catch a glimpse of the remarkable individual being introduced.

"Please join me in welcoming our esteemed guest speaker and the author of 'Forgos of the Ego,' Mark Stevenson!"

The name "Mark" didn't immediately register with Sarah and Chris. But as Mark stepped onto the stage, his familiar face triggered something in Sarah's memory.

She turned to Chris, a mix of shock and realization in her eyes. "Chris, that's... Mark."

Chris furrowed his brows in confusion, trying to make the connection. "Mark? Wait, you mean..."

Her voice trembled as she whispered, "My ex-husband. I had no idea he was the guest speaker."

Chris was taken aback, his eyes widening with surprise. "Wait, seriously? What are the odds?"

The auditorium erupted in applause, and Mark rose from his seat. Maria smiled at him, offering silent encouragement. With steady steps, he made his way to the stage, his heart a mix of emotions – gratitude, excitement, and a sense of purpose.

Alana and Michael exchanged knowing glances, their eyes filled with a blend of amusement and understanding. She, leaned over to Sarah, a smile tugging at her lips. "Looks like there's a surprise in store for you."

Her eyes widened as she looked at Alana, her voice a soft mix of shock and realization. "You knew?"

She nodded, a mischievous glint in her eyes. "I did, Sarah. Michael and I thought it would be fun to keep it a secret."

Chris joined the conversation, his voice a mix of amusement and incredulity. "So, you both knew that Mark is the guest speaker?"

Michael chimed in, his tone apologetic yet earnest. "I did, Chris. I knew you guys might not come if you knew it was Mark. But the topic is so important, and I thought it could be a chance for all of us to hear something valuable."

Alana added, her voice laced with humor, "And maybe a little unexpected twist doesn't hurt."

The applause and cheers of the audience washed over him as he stood before the podium. He took a deep breath, his gaze sweeping over the faces in the audience, appreciating the support that had brought him to this moment.

Sarah's shock gave way to a mixture of emotions, and she turned her gaze back to the stage as Mark began his speech. She couldn't help but be captivated by his words, her memories and emotions stirred by the familiar sound of his voice.

As Mark's speech resonated through the auditorium, Alana leaned in to Chris, her demeanor sympathetic. "It must be quite a surprise for both of you."

Chris nodded, a wry smile on his face. "You can say that again. But you know, the topic does seem important."

Alana nodded in agreement, her gaze shifting between Chris and the stage. "Sometimes life has a way of bringing unexpected moments to teach us something valuable."

Indeed, the irony of life was not lost on Sarah. Ever since the shared kiss in Mark's house, she had carefully avoided being alone with him. Her heart and mind were still in a state of confusion, and she didn't want to risk her emotions spiraling out of control.

As he began to speak, sharing his journey and insights, she found herself caught in a whirlwind of emotions. The past and the present collided in an unexpected twist of fate, leaving her both bewildered and intrigued. The memories they had shared, the journey they had embarked on, all seemed to resurface in this surreal moment.

Throughout his speech, she stole glances at him. The person he had become, the transformation he had undergone, was nothing short of remarkable. As he spoke eloquently about relationships and humility, she couldn't help but feel a mix of pride and nostalgia.

THIRTY-NINE

As he began his speech, the room fell into a captivated silence. Every eye was on him, eager to hear his words of wisdom.

"Ladies and gentlemen, thank you for being here today. I stand before you as someone who has learned valuable lessons about the delicate balance between success and relationships," Mark started.

Attendees leaned forward, hanging onto his every word.

"A few years ago, I went through a difficult divorce after years of marriage to the love of my life. It was a wake-up call for me, a realization that I had become so focused on my career that I neglected the most important relationships in my life," he shared.

Two attendees exchanged whispers, one saying, "I can relate to that. It's so easy to get caught up in work and forget about our loved ones."

His speech continued, his voice filled with passion and authenticity.

"I want to emphasize the importance of finding a balance between pursuing our career goals and nurturing our personal connections. It's not an easy task, but it's essential for our overall well-being and happiness," he emphasized.

An attendee nodded and said to their companion, "He's absolutely right. I've seen firsthand the toll that neglecting relationships can take on a person."

He shared practical tips and strategies for maintaining real relationships in the pursuit of success. The audience listened intently, nodding in agreement and exchanging knowing glances.

"In the end, it's not about the number of achievements or the accolades we accumulate. It's about the love, support, and connections we foster along the way. Let's remember to prioritize those relationships, to give them the time and attention they deserve," He concluded.

The room erupted into thunderous applause as attendees rose to their feet, expressing their appreciation and inspiration.

"That was incredible! I feel inspired to make changes in my own life," one attendee exclaimed, clapping enthusiastically.

Another attendee turned to their friend and said, "I never thought about it that way. He really opened my eyes to the importance of balancing work and relationships."

The auditorium was charged with anticipation as Mark's gaze swept across the room. Unexpectedly, his eyes locked with Sarah's, and his heart skipped a beat. She was the last person he had expected to see there, and yet, there she was, her presence sending a surge of emotions through him. In that fleeting moment, their eyes connected, and Mark saw a glimmer of something he hadn't witnessed in a long time—the same look she used to give him during their university days when they were deeply in love.

Mark couldn't mistake the intensity of that gaze. It was a silent invitation, a call from her eyes that resonated with the throbbing of his heart. He made a spontaneous decision to bet on the universe and seize the opportunity before him. He turned back to the audience, a determined expression on his face. "Ladies and gentlemen, if you'll indulge me, I have one more story to share before I conclude."

A hushed silence fell over the auditorium, the air charged with intrigue. Chris, seated next to Sarah, felt her gaze on him, urging him to go along with Mark's unexpected turn. He gave her an encouraging nod, his heart pounding as he sensed the weight of the moment.

As Mark began to recount his personal story of losing the love of his life, Chris followed Sarah's gaze and locked eyes with her. The look he saw in her eyes hit him like a tidal wave—a mix of nostalgia, longing, and realization. In that instant, he understood the gravity of the situation. Unconsciously, he urged her forward with a gentle nod, silently encouraging her to heed Mark's unspoken invitation.

Sarah, as if in a trance, rose from her seat and walked towards the stage. Her heart raced as the memories of their shared past flooded her mind. The room seemed to blur around her as she stepped onto the stage, her eyes never leaving Mark's. Without a word, they embraced, tears streaming down their faces, a lifetime of emotions pouring out in that single moment.

In the VIP section, Maria watched with tears in her eyes, touched by the unfolding scene. She had been witness to Mark's journey and the depths of his emotions, and now she was witnessing the culmination of it all.

Michael and Alana exchanged surprised glances, their expressions a mix of confusion and realization. Alana whispered to Michael, "Did you know about this?"

Michael shook his head, a mixture of shock and amusement on his face. "I had no idea. But it seems like fate has a way of working things out."

As Chris quietly walked out of the venue, his heart heavy with understanding, the audience remained spellbound. The collective gasp of realization rippled through the crowd, followed by a rising wave of applause and cheers. "That's her!" someone exclaimed, and the entire room rose to their feet in an endless standing ovation, clapping, shouting, and whistling in unison.

The scene on stage was a tableau of raw emotion and reconciliation, a testament to the enduring power of love. Tomorrow's newspapers and major cable networks would carry headlines of the extraordinary reunion, capturing the moment when Mark and Sarah, once separated by pride, had come full circle to find each other again.

As the sun set on that remarkable day, the world would read about the love story that had captured the hearts of those who had witnessed it. Mark and Sarah's embrace on the stage, captured in a photograph that would become iconic, would be a symbol of hope, forgiveness, and the triumph over adversity. Their story would inspire countless others to prioritize love and relationships, to let go of pride and embrace the possibilities that life had to offer.

The next day's newspapers carried the headline: "Remarkable Reunion: Love Triumphs Over Pride," accompanied by a photo of Mark and Sarah locked in an embrace on the stage. Major cable networks reported on the heartwarming reconciliation, and newspapers around the world echoed the sentiment.

EPILOGUE.

Following their remarkable journey of growth and reconciliation, Mark's professional trajectory took a remarkable turn. His newfound clarity and wisdom propelled him to climb the corporate ladder, ultimately assuming the role of CEO. He embraced his position with humility, grounded in a deep understanding of the vital balance between work and family.

As CEO, he revolutionized the workplace. His leadership was marked by transparency and compassion, prioritizing the well-being and fulfillment of his employees. He fostered an environment that encouraged open dialogue and acknowledged the intertwining of personal and professional lives. His approach resonated, inspiring others to reevaluate their priorities, ultimately contributing to a workplace defined by harmonious relationships.

Throughout their transformative journey, Sarah stood steadfastly by his side, offering invaluable advice and insights that enriched his growth as a leader and partner. As a united team, they confronted challenges and celebrated victories, navigating the intricate dance of being partners, parents, and professionals. Their bond remained unwavering, an anchor that grounded them in the importance of their connection.

Their love story continued to flourish as the years unfurled. Amid the everyday joys and milestone moments, they derived happiness from the simple pleasures of life. Their enduring marriage was founded on shared experiences, unwavering support, and an unwavering commitment to one another.

Their journey illuminated the transformative power of love, forgiveness, and personal growth. The people who crossed paths with him would forever remember his evolution from prideful to profound, a testament to the evolution of authentic connections.

Meanwhile, Chris embarked on his own journey of self-discovery and growth. Despite his family's own challenges, he had the courage to confront his actions that had inadvertently led to Mark and Sarah's reunion. Recognizing the profound history and bond between his ex-wife and Mark, Chris chose to prioritize his own well-being and happiness, navigating a path toward his unique story of fulfillment and love.

Sarah's separation from Chris was marked by kindness and mutual respect. Their respective paths diverged, both seeking individual happiness and fulfillment. Chris seized new opportunities and found love, creating a narrative that was uniquely his own.

Mark and Sarah's love story remained a testament to their enduring commitment and growth. Determined to mend their relationship, they embarked on a journey of communication, therapy, and personal improvement. Their efforts paid off, leading them to make the profound decision to remarry. Surrounded by friends and family who had witnessed their journey, their second wedding symbolized their unbreakable bond and renewed happiness, a poignant blend of emotions that spoke of a hopeful future.

Mark's role as CEO thrived, buoyed by Sarah's unwavering support and the dedication of their children. His leadership epitomized humility and was a culmination of the lessons learned on his personal journey. His influence extended beyond the professional realm, shaping a work culture that celebrated genuine relationships and individual growth.

Together, they crafted a life brimming with accomplishments, relationships, and love. They cherished each day as a precious gift, never taking their love for granted. Their story resonated deeply, a testament to the power of forgiveness, personal development, and the enduring strength of love.

With the passage of time, their bond deepened, and they forged a future characterized by happiness, fulfillment, and a profound appreciation for the significance of genuine connections. Mark's transformation from pride to humility, guided by Sarah's unwavering encouragement, underscored the truth that success transcended mere professional achievements—it was rooted in love, family, and the pursuit of authentic relationships.

Acknowledgment

Foremost, I want to express my deepest gratitude to God for His grace that enabled me to bring this novel to fruition

To my cherished family, especially my siblings Chuka, Arinze, Uchechukwu, Ifeoma, and Chinelo, your love has been my rock.

I'm immensely thankful to my mother Dame Esther Ilukwe, for instilling in me the drive to pursue my writing passion.

Finally, my friends' encouragement, my editor's guidance, and the influential authors who shaped my writing all deserve my profound appreciation. To all who contributed, your roles have made this endeavor possible, and for that, I am truly grateful.

ABOUT THE AUTHOR

Ifeanyi E. Ilukwe is a multijurisdictional lawyer licensed in Nigeria and Canada. He holds a Master's degree in Law (LLM) and is a Fellow of the Chartered Institute of Management Consultants (CIMC) in the USA and Nigeria. With expertise in law, management consulting, and project management, Ifeanyi provides exceptional legal services and valuable insights to clients across different jurisdictions. He is also a distinguished author, known for his book "Judicial Interpretation of Words, Phrases, and Legal Maxims in Nigeria: Ilukwe's Dictionary of Legal Terms." Ifeanyi's professionalism, integrity, and commitment to excellence make him a trusted legal professional, consultant, and author.